# Abbie an' Slats

**Volume 2**

*Featuring* **BATHLESS GROGGINS**

*by* **RAEBURN VAN BUREN**

U. S. CLASSICS SERIES (TM). ABBIE an' SLATS ©1941 through 1964 by United Feature Syndicate.
Reprinted by permission of Raeburn Van Buren.
Introduction ©1984 by Herb Galewitz. Special thanks to Chuck Ager.
Published by Ken Pierce, Inc., P.O. Box 332, Park Forest, Illinois 60466.
Complete lists for a stamp.

ISBN: 0-912277-24-6

"I used to buy India ink by the quart." —*Raeburn Van Buren.*
While involved in the production of this second volume of *Abbie an' Slats*, Ken Pierce suggested I take my trusty camera with me the next time I visited Van. Above is the result (summer, 1984). Van will be celebrating his 93rd birthday in January of 1985!

# Sunday mornings with Bathless Groggins...

By 1941 *Abbie an' Slats* had been rolling along for almost four years, and during this time the dailies and Sundays had been intertwined. (The Sunday page was actually launched some time after the dailies originated in August, 1937.) But now the newspapers were filled with depressing war news about Nazi conquered Europe and the expansionist activities of Japan in the Pacific.

United Feature Syndicate, who distributed the strip, felt that the public was ripe for more escapist fare. They let their feelings be known to Al Capp and Raeburn Van Buren, who were collaborating on the feature. In the main, *Abbie an' Slats* had concerned itself with the romantic escapades of Slats and Beckie, with comic relief supplied by Abbie and Bathless (see our first volume).

Al and Van felt the suggestion was valid and they decided to turn the Sunday page into a Bathless Groggins farrago. No longer was he to be Pop, the mellow old codger, but rather a tough yet quixotic old curmudgeon who had sown his wild oats as a young man in worldwide escapades that could now be retold in a Baron Munchausen fashion.

Our second volume of *Abbie an' Slats* devotes itself to those Bathless Groggins Sunday pages where Al Capp's imagination and Raeburn Van Buren's gifted pen let comedy be supreme. We have an array of sixteen stories ranging from 1941 through 1964. (The latter stories were written by Elliott Caplin.) There are tales of improbable maharajahs, zany inventions, odd boxing matches, and encounters with two of the best supporting players, Jasper Hagstone, the millionaire you love to hate, and Haggis McBagpipe, the Scotch pig farmer with the formidable moustache.

Through all the slapstick these Sunday pages bear one characteristic in common with the dailies, and that is that Al and Van made sure that not too many episodes went by without a pretty girl gracing the page. If there were no female leads in a paticular story, that was no reason not to depict a passing beauty or a dancing girl in the background. Their presence may not have advanced the storyline, but " a thing of beauty is a joy for ever." Keats, Capp, Van Buren and many comic strip fans say *Amen* to that!

ABBIE an' SLATS
by RAEBURN VAN BUREN

ALL THESE BIRDS ARE FAKES! HMM—TH' POOLROOM IS CLOSED FOR REPAIRS TODAY AFTER LAST NIGHT'S FREE-FOR-ALL--SO I'LL PERFORM A PUBLIC SERVICE BY EXPOSIN' THIS PHONY!

MOST OF CRABTREE CORNERS' UPPER-CRUST ARE PRESENT AT THE SWAMI'S SUITE AT THE MANSION HOUSE HOTEL.
THE SWAMI WILL CONSENT TO SEE ONLY A LIMITED NUMBER. I'LL TAKE YOUR CARDS IN.
I AIN'T GOT A CARD. ALL I GOT WITH MY NAME ON IT—IS THIS MEMBERSHIP CARD IN THE GARBAGE SCOW PILOTS ASSOCIATION-- LOCAL NO. 13!!

MR. GROGGINS— FIRST!
WELL—BLARST MY EYES! ("MAYBE HE KNOWS I KNOW HE'S A FAKE—AND HE WANTS TO BRIBE ME TO CLAM UP!")

IF HE THINKS A FEW DOLLARS CAN BUY ME OFF, HE'S CRAZY. I GOT IDEALS. IT'LL TAKE AT LEAST TEN!
Copr. 1948 by United Feature Syndicate, Inc.
Tm. Reg. U. S. Pat. Off.—All rights reserved

GROGGINS! THERE IS A PECULIAR AURA ABOUT YOU!
DON'T GET PERSONAL, PAL!

I DIDN'T SAY AROMA— I SAID AURA. AN AURA OF DOUBT— AND SKEPTICISM!
KEERECT! BUT I WON'T SAY A WORD TO THOSE SUCKERS OUT THERE IF YOU READS MY PALM WITH A TEN-SPOT!

YOU DO DOUBT. AHHH-- I SEE BY YOUR PALM YOU WERE NOT ALWAYS A GRIMY OLD MAN. YOU WERE ONCE A GRIMY YOUNG MAN!
R. Van Buren

I SEE A HIGH-WALLED TURKESTAN DWELLING. I SEE A YOUNG, AGILE, RED-HEADED SAILOR, WITH A CERTAIN LIGHT IN HIS EYE—HELPING A BEAUTIFUL, IF SLIGHTLY OVERWEIGHT, VEILED YOUNG LADY CLIMB DOWN A LADDER FROM A BARRED HAREM WINDOW!
3/14

WAITING OUTSIDE IS HIS PAL —A FINE-LOOKING, DARK-EYED, WELL-BUILT, YOUNG LAD!
THIS IS UNCANNY!

SUDDENLY THERE IS A ROAR FROM TH' HAREM! THE GIRL'S FATHER APPEARS —SLICING THE NIGHT AIR WITH A GLEAMING SCIMITAR! OH, THAT WAS A CLOSE ONE, GROGGINS— BUT--HA, HA— WE ESCAPED!
WE??
TO BE CONTINUED"

HAD YOU FOOLED AT FIRST -- EH, GROGGINS?
SCARED TH' BEJABBERS OUTA ME! I COULDA SWORE NOBODY IN TH' WORLD KNEW ABOUT THAT HAREM DEAL IN TURKESTAN, THIRTY YEARS AGO, EXCEPT ME, FAT FATIMA, AN' MY OLE PAL, SAMMY. NEVER FIGURED YOU'D CHANGE YOUR NAME TO SWAMI-- AND YOUR BUSINESS FROM PALMIN' CARDS TO READIN' PALMS!

IT'S A GREAT LI'L RACKET, BATHLESS -- YOU JUST TELLS 'EM VAGUE THINGS THAT'S TRUE ABOUT ANYBODY-- THAT GETS 'EM TRUSTIN' YOU -- GETS 'EM TALKIN' THEMSELVES!

FROM THERE ON IN IT'S A PUSHOVER. BEFORE THEY'VE REALIZED IT-- THEY'VE TOLD YOU ALL ABOUT THEMSELVES--AND THEY THINK IT'S WONDERFUL THAT YOU KNOW EVERYTHING THERE IS TO KNOW ABOUT 'EM!

FOR THIS--THEY PAY THROUGH THE NOSE AND WORSHIP ME. IT'S PITIFUL-- TH' FAITH THEY HAVE IN ME! THEY'LL DO ANYTHING I ADVISE 'EM TO DO!

SWAMI -- YOUR NEXT CLIENT IS -- MR. JASPER HAGSTONE!
OLD PAL, THIS IS THE OPPORTUNITY OF A LIFETIME! LEND ME THAT TURBAN--AND DIM TH' LIGHTS.

FIFTEEN MINUTES WITH HAGSTONE--AND I'M MADE FOR LIFE!
TAKE YOUR TIME, BATHLESS. IS THERE A POOLROOM NEAR BY?

SWAMI! I'M A HARD-HEADED, PRACTICAL MAN. I'LL COME RIGHT TO THE POINT! FRANKLY, I DOUBT THAT YOU CAN TELL ME ANYTHING ABOUT ME FROM MY PALM! I'M NO ORDINARY FOOL!
YOU SURE AIN'T, SAHIB!
3/21

I WANT PROOF OF YOUR POWERS. TELL ME SOMETHING ABOUT MYSELF!
I SEE HATE! NO MEAN, MISERABLE, NAMBY-PAMBY HATE, BUT A HATE THAT IS BIGGER AND STRONGER THAN ANY OTHER EMOTION YOU HAVE!

DAY AND NIGHT-- YOU THINK OF NOTHING ELSE BUT WAYS TO DEGRADE AND DEMOLISH THE OBJECT OF THIS GREAT HATRED OF YOURS-- ONE WHO IS CALLED, GROGGINS!
YOU'RE RIGHT, SWAMI! ABSOLUTELY RIGHT! NOW I HAVE FAITH-- I BELIEVE!
TO BE CONTINUED

IT'S UNCANNY—HOW RIGHT YOU ARE, SWAMI! I AM CONSUMED WITH HATE! A RED-HOT, SIZZLING HATE. FOR GROGGINS!
IT IS WRITTEN IN YOUR PALM, SAHIB!

AND DOES MY PALM ALSO REVEAL SOME WAY TO DEMOLISH AND DESTROY THIS OBSTACLE TO MY HAPPINESS? THIS GROGGINS!
AH, YES!

A PAINFUL WAY, I HOPE, AN AGONIZING WAY! BUT A WAY THAT WON'T GET ME INTO ANY TROUBLE. THE MORE FIENDISH IT IS, TH' MORE I'LL ENJOY IT!
TSK, TSK, TSK!

THAT'S THE WAY WITH YOU WESTERN BARBARIANS! YOU CAN THINK OF NO WAY TO ATTACK YOUR ENEMIES--EXCEPT WITH CRUDE CRUELTY!
AND THAT'S WRONG ???

FIGURE IT OUT FOR YOURSELF, SAHIB! YOU'VE SPENT YOUR ENTIRE LIFE ATTACKING GROGGINS WITH TH' CRUDEST SORT OF CRUELTY--AND YET--HE LAUGHS AT YOU!

HA, HA, HA, HA! LIKE THAT!
EGAD! IT'S UNCANNY! IT SOUNDED LIKE GROGGINS LAUGHING AT ME!

HAVE YOU EVER BROODED OVER THAT SUBTLE FAR EASTERN PHRASE-- "KILL WITH KINDNESS" ????
I DON'T CARE HOW I DO IT! IF THAT'S A BETTER SYSTEM, SWAMI--I'M FOR IT! HOW'LL I GO ABOUT IT?

SHOWER TH' RAT WITH GIFTS! GIVE HIM EVERYTHING HIS WICKED OLD HEART DESIRES. SHARE ALL YOUR EARTHLY POSSESSIONS WITH HIM!
I DON'T UNDERSTAND YOUR ADVICE, SWAMI-- BUT I'VE GOT FAITH IN YOU-- SO I'LL TAKE IT!

I'LL KILL GROGGINS YOUR WAY-- WITH KINDNESS! EVEN IF IT TAKES EVERYTHING I'VE GOT! HO, HO, HO, HO, HA, HA, HA, HA!

HO, HO, HO, HA, HA, HA!
TO BE CONTINUED

THANKS A MILLION FOR TH' LOAN OF TH' TURBAN AN' TH' CRYSTAL BALL, SWAMI! OH—HO! HO! HO! DID I PULL A FAST ONE ON THAT FAT RAT, HAGSTONE!

HE DIDN'T RECOGNIZE ME--THOUGHT I WAS YOU. SO I TELLS HIM TH' ONLY WAY TO GET TH' MAN HE HATES—THAT'S ME—WAS T' STOP ABUSING HIM AN' ATTACKING HIM--

--BUT—T' SHOWER ME WITH GIFTS INSTEAD. T' GIVE ME EVERYTHING MY WICKED OLD HEART DESIRES. IN OTHER WORDS, SWAMI, OLD PAL, I TOLD HIM—HA, HA, HA--KILL ME WITH KINDNESS!
YOU TOLD HIM THAT, GROGGINS?

YOU FOOL! YOU'VE SIGNED YOUR OWN DEATH WARRANT!
HUH?

AS YOU KNOW, I'M A PHONY. I DON'T KNOW ANYTHING ABOUT HINDU TYPE PHILOSOPHY-- EXCEPT ONE THING--

AND THAT IS —THAT THE SUREST WAY TO KILL AN ENEMY IS TO KILL HIM WITH KINDNESS! I BEG OF YOU, BATHLESS, OLD PAL —

CONFESS TO HAGSTONE INSTANTLY-- THAT IT WAS ALL A HOAX! CONFESS! BEFORE HE BEGINS TO SHOWER YOU WITH GIFTS AND —
WHAT? TALK MYSELF OUTA ALL THAT-- JUST AFTER I TALKS MYSELF INTO IT?

MARK MY WORDS, BATHLESS — IF YOU GO ON WITH THIS MAD PLAN YOU WILL BE KILLED WITH KINDNESS!
DON'T BE SILLY! SO LONG, PAL — FROM NOW ON IT'S TH' EASY LIFE FOR ME!
Copr. 1948 by United Feature Syndicate, Inc.
Tm. Reg. U. S. Pat. Off.—All rights reserved
4-4

YOUR CAR IS WAITING, MR. GROGGINS. COMPLIMENTS OF MR. HAGSTONE. MY NAME IS WORMLEY, SIR!
— HOME, WORMLEY!

THIS MANSION AIN'T MY HOME, WORMLEY!
IT IS NOW, SIR. COMPLIMENTS OF MR. HAGSTONE!
TO BE CONTINUED

IN THE GUISE OF A HINDU SWAMI, POP, HIMSELF, ADVISED HAGSTONE THAT THE SUREST WAY TO DESTROY HIS WORST ENEMY, (POP, HIMSELF), WAS TO "KILL HIM WITH KINDNESS"! POP, HIMSELF, IS NOW REAPING THE REWARDS OF HIS CUNNING······
MINE! ALL MINE — AN' HAGSTONE IS PAYIN' FOR IT!

OH WHAT A FOOL TH' REAL SWAMI WAS, WARNIN' ME THAT A MAN ACTUALLY COULD KILL HIS WORST ENEMY WITH KINDNESS! I FEEL GREAT!!

LUNCHEON, SIR. PRESSED DUCK, CAVIAR, SEA FOOD A LA LITTLE CLUB, BREAST OF PHEASANT A LA STORK CLUB, AND LA GRANDE DESSERT A LA ROYAL. COMPLIMENTS OF MR. HAGSTONE!
AHHHH-HHHH!

THIS IS A LOT FINER THAN MY CUSTOMARY DOUGHNUTS AN' COFFEE WHICH I USED TO GET ON TH' CUFF AT JOE'S BEANERY!

BUT - (CHOKE!) - - IT'S TOO GOOD AND TOO MUCH - - AND IT ALL CAME TOO EASY!

I GUESS I'LL GO OVER T' TH' POOLROOM AN' TRY T' TALK BUD TINGLE INTO LETTIN' ME SHOOT A COUPLA GAMES O' KELLY POOL ON CREDIT!

BUT - - ??? I GOT FOUR POOL TABLES RIGHT HERE! I CAN PLAY FOR FREE. BUT SOMEHOW — NOW - - I DON'T WANTA! IT'S TOO EASY!
Copr. 1948 by United Feature Syndicate, Inc.
Tm. Reg. U. S. Pat. Off. —All rights reserved

A FEW DAYS LATER···
THE MASTER JUST SITS THERE, DOCTOR - - HE LOOKS ILL — LIFELESS — GREEN AROUND THE GILLS!
HMMM - - -
4-11

THERE IS SOMETHING WRONG, BUT IT DEFIES MEDICAL DIAGNOSIS. I'D BETTER CALL A PSYCHIATRIST!

BAD! VERY BAD! THERE'S NO WILL TO GO ON. AND YET — HE HAS EVERYTHING! HMMM — THIS MAN - IS BEING KILLED BY KINDNESS!!
TO BE CONTINUED

IN ALL MY CAREER AS A PSYCHIATRIST— I'VE NEVER SEEN A MAN IN SUCH ROTTEN SHAPE. YOU'VE LOST THE WILL TO DO ANYTHING AT ALL. EVEN TO EAT! YOU'RE OBVIOUSLY SUFFERING FROM MALNUTRITION, MR GROGGINS. WHY DON'T YOU EAT?
I USED T' LOVE T' EAT-- WHEN I COULD SOFT-SOAP SOMEBODY INTO STAKIN' ME TO A MEAL!

BUT ALL THIS STUFF — COMES TOO EASY! IT'S TOO BLARSTED GOOD AN' THERE'S TOO MUCH OF IT! I — JUST — AIN'T — INTERESTED!
YOU NEED EXERCISE, BADLY!

SIGHH! I USED T' GIT PLENTY O' EXERCISE — SPRINTIN' AWAY FROM CRAP GAMES — WHEN THEY WAS RAIDED!

ALSO LOTS O' PUNCHIN'-BAG TYPE EXERCISE WHEN TH' BOYS AT TH' CLUB GOT MELLOW. PLENTY O' SHOULDER AN' CHEST STUFF TOO — WHEN I GOT PUSHED OFF CORNERS FOR LOITERIN'!

BUT— NOW— I'M A RICH MAN. EVERYBODY RESPECTS ME. NOBODY SLUGS ME OR SHOVES ME AROUND. (SIGH!) ALL I HAFTA DO IS SIT HERE!

SURROUNDED BY (SIGH!) EVERY COMFORT AN' LUXURY!
WHO IS RESPONSIBLE FOR ALL THIS SUDDEN GOOD FORTUNE? A DEAR FRIEND?
4-18

NO! JASPER HAGSTONE-- MY WORST ENEMY!
AHHH— THAT EXPLAINS IT! HOW DIABOLICALLY CLEVER OF HIM! HE IS KILLING YOU WITH KINDNESS! AN ANCIENT AND HIDEOUS HINDU METHOD OF VENGEANCE. YOUR CONDITION IS HOPELESS! I'LL SEND MY BILL TO HAGSTONE

BATHLESS, OLD PAL! LOOK WHAT FLEW IN FROM HAVANA FOR YOU-- THE RAREST OF ALL CIGARS — EL AROMA DE ASHCANNOS
YA DIABOLICALLY CLEVER RAT!

SO NOW YA WANTS T' TAKE AWAY MY ONE REMAININ' PLEASURE — SMOKIN'!!!!
BAP!

IT'S GREAT T' BE ON MY OWN AGAIN. NOW LIFE'S WORTH LIVIN'!

ABBIE an' SLATS by
RAEBURN VAN BUREN

THE INTELLIGENCE DEPARTMENT OF THE UNITED NATIONS, FAR EASTERN COMMAND--------
AS YOU SEE, THE MAHARA-JAHDOM OF POOLPAHLAH IS SITUATED IN AN EXTREMELY VITAL SPOT. THE SUCCESS OF OUR CAMPAIGN DEPENDS ON US GETTING THE MAHARAJAH'S PERMISSION TO USE POOLPAHLAH RIVER TO CONVEY OUR SUPPLIES--

THE MAHARAJAH IS A DIFFICULT, ECCENTRIC CHAP. HE REFUSES TO SEE THE AGENTS OF EITHER OUR SIDE OR THE ENEMY. IN FACT-- HE IS COMPLETELY INACCESSIBLE---- AND REFUSES TO GIVE ANY DEFINITE ANSWER. MEANWHILE, PRECIOUS TIME IS PASSING
CAN'T WE PUT PRESSURE ON HIM?

IMPOSSIBLE!!! NO ONE CAN EVEN GET TO HIM!!
HMM--- IF ONLY WE KNEW OF SOMEONE FOR WHOM HE HAS AFFECTION-- SOMEONE TO WHOM HE IS INDEBTED!!

(SIGH!!) WE'VE EXAMINED THE RECORD OF HIS WHOLE LIFE. HE IS INDEBTED TO NO ONE!! HE HAS NO AFFECTION FOR ANY HUMAN BEING!! READ THE RECORD YOURSELF!!
HMMM--- WHAT'S THIS?

"IN THE SUMMER OF 1913 THE MAHARAJAH WAS SAVED FROM BEING CLAWED TO DEATH BY A WILD TIGER-- BY AN AMERICAN SAILOR WHO, IN RESCUING THE MAHARAJAH, WAS MAIMED IN A PECULIARLY EMBARRASSING MANNER"----

NOW--- THERE IS A MAN FOR WHOM EVEN THE COLD-BLOODED MAHARAJAH MUST CERTAINLY HAVE SOME AFFECTION! A MAN TO WHOM HE IS CERTAINLY INDEBTED!!
(SIGH!!) AH, YES--- BUT NO CLUE EXISTS AS TO THE IDENTITY OF THAT AMERICAN SAILOR. READ ON!

"--AS A REWARD, THE MAHARAJAH OFFERED THE AMERICAN SAILOR HALF OF HIS WEALTH AND HALF OF HIS HAREM OF ONE THOUSAND BEAUTIFUL WIVES. THESE WERE TO BE PRESENTED TO THE SAILOR IMMEDIATELY AFTER THE CEREMONIAL DINNER----"
MAY-24
Copr. 1942 by United Feature Syndicate, Inc.
Tm. Reg. U. S. Pat. Off.—All rights reserved
R. VAN BUREN

"-- THE MAHARAJAH WAITED FOR HIS GUEST TO BEGIN THE CEREMONIAL DINNER--- BUT THE GUEST NEVER TURNED UP. HE VANISHED AND WAS NEVER SEEN IN POOLPAHLAH AGAIN!!"
GREAT SCOTT!! WHY DIDN'T HE TURN UP AT THE DINNER?

I'VE BEEN TO THEM MYSELF---THEY'RE WONDERFUL. THEY BEGIN--- WITH A BATH--- FOLLOWED BY---
BY JOVE!! THAT'S IT!! THAT SAILOR GAVE UP HALF A MAHARAJAHDOM-- A HAREM OF FIVE HUNDRED BEAUTIFUL WIVES RATHER THAN TAKE A BATH!

IF WE CAN FIND AN AMERICAN SAILOR WHO HATES BATHS ENOUGH TO MAKE THAT SACRIFICE, WE'VE GOT OUR MAN!!
TO BE CONTINUED---

CONTINUED FROM LAST WEEK---
ARE YOU GROGGINS, FORMERLY FIRST MATE OF THE TRAMP STEAMER, "SIMPLE SUE"?
STEP INTO THE NEXT ROOM, PLEASE, SIR
KEERECT!

AHA! THERE THEY ARE -- THE TIGER CLAW MARKS
KEERECT! GOT THEM 30 YEARS AGO SAVIN' THE MAHARAJAH OF POOLPAHLAH

EXACTLY AND, AS A REWARD, THE MAHARAJAH WAS TO GIVE YOU HALF HIS KINGDOM AND HALF HIS HAREM--500 BEAUTIFUL GIRLS!!
BUT THE RECORDS SHOW YOU NEVER TURNED UP FOR THE PRESENTATION DINNER. MAY I ASK WHY?
BECAUSE THE BLARSTED THING BEGAN WITH A BATH, THAT'S WHY!!

YOU'RE OUR MAN, GROGGINS. EVERYTHING CHECKS WITH THE RECORD. POOLPAHLAH IS NOW VITALLY IMPORTANT TO THE SUCCESS OF THE CAMPAIGN---
WE MUST GET THE MAHARAJAH'S PERMISSION TO USE THE RIVER BUT SO FAR HE REFUSES TO SEE ANYONE!
Copr. 1942 by United Feature Syndicate, Inc.
Tm. Reg. U. S. Pat. Off.—All rights reserved

YOU, GROGGINS, ARE THE ONE MAN WHO CAN GET TO THE MAHARAJAH. WILL YOU TRY?
HERE ARE INSTRUCTIONS, TICKETS AND MONEY-- LOTS OF LUCK!
KEERECT!

THREE WEEKS LATER---
POOLPAHLAH IS 20 MILES AWAY. WE WILL HURRY AND REACH IT IN EIGHT DAYS
THAT'S WHAT I LIKE, KID-- SPEED!!

THERE HE IS, HONORABLE COMMANDER!!
I WILL DROP HONORABLE BOMB ON DISHONORABLE HIM---
R. VAN BUREN

BANZAI!!
5-31

BUT WHY STOP OUR SLAVE CARAVAN FOR THIS MISERABLE CARCASS?
I DOUBT IF HE WOULD BRING MORE THAN A DROOPEE IN A FIRE SALE
I MERELY THOUGHT MASTERS, THAT WE COULD GIVE HIM AWAY FREE AS A SORT OF SALES INDUCER!
TO BE CONTINUED-----

OH, NO, GROTESQUE ONE--YOU ARE NOT IN HEAVEN!! YOU ARE IN THE POOLPAHLAH SLAVE QUARTERS AWAITING, AS WE ALL ARE, TO BE SOLD ON THE AUCTION BLOCK
THEY CAN'T DO THAT T'ME--- I'M AN AMERICAN CITIZEN!!--BATHLESS GROGGINS, THEY CALLS ME, AND SMALL WONDER!! I'M ON AN IMPORTANT MISSION FOR THE UNITED NATIONS. I'VE GOT TO GET TO MY OLD PAL, THE MAHARAJAH OF POOLPAHLAH!!
HERE THEY COME FOR US

LOT NUMBER 5 COMING UP!
TAKE THESE CHAINS OFF OF ME, YOU LUGS!! AND BRING ME TO MY FRIEND, THE MAHARAJAH!

QUIET!!
OUCH!! YA SEA-APE--O!!--YA YELLOW-LIVERED--!!

AND HERE, GOOD CITIZENS--IS THE BEST BUY IN TOWN!! LOT NUMBER 5 INCLUDES NOT ONLY THE USUAL DOZEN BEAUTIFUL DANCING GIRLS--BUT--AS AN EXTRA ADDED ATTRACTION--

WE ARE GIVING AWAY--ABSOLUTELY FREE--THIS LAUGHABLE CARICATURE OF A HUMAN BEING!! NOTE WELL THE HUMOROUS REMARKS HE IS ABOUT TO MAKE----
Copr. 1942 by United Feature Syndicate, Inc.
Tm. Reg. U. S. Pat. Off.—All rights reserved

OUCH!! YA #!! SEA-APE--O!! YA YELLOW-LIVERED----!!
HO HO!!

BOTH THE **UNITED NATIONS** AND THE **AXIS** ARE DESPERATELY ANXIOUS TO WIN THE ECCENTRIC **MAHARAJAH** OF **POOLPAHLAH** TO THEIR SIDE. BUT THE POTENTATE REFUSES TO SEE AGENTS OF **EITHER SIDE!!**

POP, WHO SAVED THE MAHARAJAH 30 YEARS AGO FROM A TIGER, HAS BEEN SENT AS AN AGENT OF THE UNITED NATIONS. NOW THROUGH A SERIES OF MISFORTUNES POP HAS ARRIVED IN POOLPAHLAH-- **SOLD AS A SLAVE**, AND A CHEAP ONE AT THAT.

THE TWO GENTLEMEN PICTURED ARE THE AXIS AGENTS, WHO, THUS FAR, HAVE BEEN UNABLE TO GET TO THE MAHARAJAH........

OH, BATHLESS ONE!! AFTER 30 YEARS I'VE FOUND YOU!! ONCE YOU SAVED MY LIFE---THEN VANISHED BEFORE I COULD REWARD YOU! I WILL DO ANYTHING IN MY POWER FOR YOU, OH, MAGNIFICENTLY UNSANITARY ONE!!
THAT'S MIGHTY WHITE O'YOU, PAL!!

I HAVE A FAVOR TO ASK, PAL-- BUT IT'S A FAVOR I DON'T WANT YOU TO DO JUST FOR ME!!! I WANT YOU TO JUDGE THE WHOLE THING ON ITS MERITS!!! THERE'S A WAR GOING ON YOU KNOW
SO THEY TELL ME, OH, YOU OF A THOUSAND INDESCRIBABLE PERFUMES!

THERE'S TWO SIDES. THE AXIS--AND THE UNITED NATIONS.!! BOTH WANT TO USE YOUR MAHARAJAHDOM TO TRANSPORT SUPPLIES
AH, YES!! BUT I HAVE REFUSED TO BE BOTHERED. HOWEVER, BECAUSE OF MY GREAT LOVE FOR YOU--OH, YOU WITH THE DUST OF MANY NATIONS ON YOUR HIDE--

I WILL GIVE THE USE OF MY MAHARAJAHDOM TO YOUR SIDE, WHICH-EVER IT IS!! SPEAK!!
THANKS PAL--BUT I WANT YOU TO DO THIS--- NOT ON ACCOUNT O'ME--BUT ON ACCOUNT YOU BELIEVE MY SIDE IS RIGHT! I WON'T EVEN TELL YOU WHICH SIDE I'M ON. I'LL JUST TELL YOU WHAT EACH SIDE BELIEVES IN!!

AND I'M SURE A MAN O' YOUR INTELLIGENCE WILL DECIDE IN FAVOR O' THE RIGHT SIDE.!!
NATURALLY-- SPEAK!!

THE UNITED NATIONS ARE FIGHTIN' FOR FREEDOM!! FIGHTIN' FOR THE RIGHTS O'ALL HUMAN BEIN'S--BIG AN' SMALL--OF ALL NATIONS AN' FAITHS--TO LIVE, WORK AN' WORSHIP IN THEIR OWN WAY-- THAT'S ONE SIDE---

THEN--THERE'S THE OTHER SIDE-- THEY'RE FIGHTIN' TO KEEP JUST A FEW GUYS ON TOP-- TO KEEP THE REST O'MANKIND AS SLAVES--TO LIVE, WORK AN' WORSHIP AS THEIR MASTERS TELL 'EM. THAT'S THE AXIS SIDE. NOW WHICH SIDE ARE YOU ON, PAL ?
THE AXIS SIDE, OF COURSE !! A FEW LIKE ME AND YOU--ON TOP-- THE REST--- SLAVES!-- SPLENDID IDEA !!
Copr. 1942 by United Feature Syndicate, Inc.
Tm. Reg. U. S. Pat. Off.—All rights reserved

NATURALLY-- THAT'S YOUR SIDE!! I WILL CALL IN MY MINISTERS AT ONCE--AND PROCLAIM THAT THE USE OF MY MAHARAJAHDOM GOES TO THAT WONDERFUL AXIS
NO-NO!! HOLD IT, PAL !!!

YOU'VE GOTTA BE EDUCATED, PAL !! I'VE GOTTA PROVE TO YOU THAT A FEW BIG GUYS HAVIN' THE RIGHT TO KICK AROUND MILLIONS O'LITTLE GUYS-- IS DEAD WRONG!!
BUT THAT IS THE ONLY SENSIBLE THEORY, IT SEEMS TO ME, O'BEGRIMED ONE!!!
R. VAN BUREN
JUNE -21
TO BE CONTINUED ------

CONTINUED FROM LAST WEEK-- MAHARAJAH, OLE PAL--I'M GONNA PROVE TO YOU THAT THE AXIS THEORY THAT A FEW BIG GUYS IN THE WORLD HAVE GOT ANY RIGHT TO KICK AROUND THE MILLIONS O'LITTLE GUYS--IS DEAD WRONG!!
BUT, OH, BATHLESS ONE-- THAT IS THE ONLY SENSIBLE THEORY!!

AFTER ALL--SOME OF US ARE BORN SUPERIOR---LIKE, FOR INSTANCE-- ME. AND SOME ARE BORN INFERIOR--LIKE ALL THE REST OF THE PEOPLE IN MY MAHARAJAHDOM!
THERE'S NOTHIN' SUPERIOR ABOUT YOU, OLE PAL--EXCEPT THE POWER AND THE CROWN YOU INHERITED--

TAKE THAT POWER AND THAT CROWN AWAY--AND YOU'RE JUST A LUG LIKE ANYONE ELSE!!
NONSENSE!! MY SUPERIOR- ITY IS SOME- THING THAT CAN'T BE TAKEN AWAY FROM ME-- THAT CAN'T BE HIDDEN!! AH-H-H IF ONLY I COULD PROVE IT TO YOU!

YOU SURE CAN--BY SHEDDIN' ALL THEM FANCY CLOTHES, DRES- SIN' IN RAGS, AND MINGLIN' WITH THE COMMON HERD
OF COURSE!! AND YOU WITH THE DUST OF MANY NATIONS ON YOUR HIDE, WILL SEE THAT MY SUPERIORITY OVER THESE INFERIOR CREATURES WILL BE INSTANTLY RECOGNIZED!!

WELL?
WELL WHAT?

SALAAM, YOU SON OF A SERPENT AND A BABOON!! SALAAM!!

AHA!!JUST AS I SUSPECTED!! NOT A SINGLE DROOPEE ON EITHER OF YOU!! YOU ARE FAMILIAR WITH OUR NOBLE MAHARAJAH'S NEW LAW, OF COURSE?
OF COURSE NOT!! I NEVER READ 'EM-- I JUST SIGN 'EM!! THE DETAILS ARE ATTENDED TO BY MY MINISTERS

ENOUGH OF YOUR RAVINGS, O'PITIFUL ONE WITH DELU- SIONS OF GRANDEUR!! THE NEW LAW STATES THAT ANY- ONE FOUND ON THE STREETS OF POOLPAHLAH WITHOUT, AT LEAST, THREE DROOPEES-- IS SOLD INTO SLAVERY TO PAY THE FINE!!
3 DROOPEES
3 DROOPEES
6 DROOPEES
RECONDITIONED ALSO NEW RETREADS GOOD FOR ANOTHER THOUSAND MILES 6 DROOPEES!
TO BE CONTINUED--
JUNE-28
R. VanBuren-

AND SO, Y'SEE, MAHARAJAH, OLE PAL-- THE AXIS THEORY THAT A LOT O' BIG FELLAS ARE SO SUPERIOR THEY'VE GOT THE RIGHT TO KICK AROUND ALL THE LITTLE FELLAS IN THE WORLD IS -- DEAD WRONG!!
3 DROOPEES
3 DROOPEES
6 DROOPEES

YOU WERE ONE O'THE BIG SUPERIOR FELLAS, UNTIL YOU SHED YOUR FANCY CLOTHES. IN RAGS YOU'RE A SLAVE WORTH HALF AS MUCH AS THAT MULE. WHERE'S YOUR SUPERIOR-ITY NOW?
WOE IS ME!! I HAVE LEARNED A GREAT LESSON. TRULY ALL MEN ARE CREATED EQUAL

THE TWO AXIS AGENTS APPROACH----
(GROAN !!) THE MA-HARAJAH STILL REFUSES TO MAKE HIS DECISION AS TO WHICH SIDE CAN USE THIS MAHARAJAH-DOM FOR MILITARY PURPOSES!!
LOOK !! THAT SLAVE GREATLY RESEMBLES IN HIS INFERIOR WAY-- THE NOBLE MAHARAJAH!! I HAVE A TREMEN DOUS IDEA!! BUY HIM - QUICKLY!!

THE HOME OF THE AXIS AGENTS--
BUT CURSE YOUR HIDES-- I AM THE MAHARAJAH-- OUCH!!
HA! HA! NOT ONLY DOES THIS LOWLY DOG RESEMBLE THE MAHARAJAH-- HE ALSO TAKES ON HIS HIGH AND MIGHTY AIRS!!
SLAVE! LISTEN TO YOUR MASTER!

IN A FEW MINUTES-- THE MAHARAJAH'S PALACE WILL BE BLOWN UP BY OUR MEN. AS THE POPULACE MOURNS ITS LOST RULER-- WE WILL ANNOUNCE THAT, FORTUNATELY, HE WAS VISITING US WHEN THE EXPLOSION TOOK PLACE

WE WILL THEN PRESENT YOU, DOG AS THE MAHARAJAH, AND FROM THEN ON--- YOU TAKE ORDERS FROM US !!
YOUR FIRST ORDER WILL BE TO TURN YOUR HA-HA-MAHARA-JAHDOM OVER TO THE AXIS FOR MILITARY PURPOSES

ONCE WE TAKE OVER--WE WILL TREAT ALL YOU INFERIOR SWINE JUST AS WE TREAT THE REST OF THE WORLD! YOU WILL HAVE THE PRIVILEGE OF SERVING US, YOUR NATURAL BORN MASTERS, AND NO OTHER PRIVILEGES!

THERE GOES THE PALACE!!
BOOM!

ONE HOUR LATER-- SLAVE MARKET
THAT TREACHEROUS SLAVE !! ONCE WE CONVINCED THE POPULACE THAT HE WAS THE MAHARAJAH-- HIS FIRST ACT WAS TO CAST US INTO SLAVERY !!
PRICE ONE DROOPEE
PRICE ONE DROOPEE
PRICE 8 DROOPEES
7-5

I HAVE JUST ABOLISHED SLAVERY IN MY MAHARAJAHDOM, EXCEPT FOR THOSE TWO GERMANS, OF COURSE-- AND I AM NOW GOING TO CALL UP MY ARMY TO JOIN THE UNITED NATIONS IN ABOL-ISHING SLAVERY ALL OVER THE WORLD!
ABOLISH SLAVERY ALL OVER THE WORLD IS KEERECT!!

ABBIE an' SLATS by
RAEBURN VAN BUREN

SO YOU'RE OFF TO TOOKERVILLE FOR THE REUNION OF THE OLD CREW OF THE S.S. ANNIE ANANIAS!
KEERECT!! EVERY FIVE YEARS US BOYS GETS TOGETHER AND HAS A LI'L CELEBRATION.

A WORSE BUNCH O' BARE-FACED LIARS NEVER SAILED THE SEAS!! THERE ISN'T A WORD O' TRUTH IN ANY OF 'EM—NEVER WAS!!!

HOW'VE YOU BEEN DOING LATELY?
CAN'T KICK!! JUST SOLD MY FLEET O' SHIPS TO THE GOVERNMENT!! DIDN'T MAKE A CENT O' PROFIT—SIMPLY TOOK WHAT THEY WERE WORTH, A MILLION!
IT AIN'T BIG DOUGH—BUT ITS A LIVIN'!
SO YOU CORNERED THE STOCK MARKET AGAIN, EH? BUT AIN'T THAT THE SAME PAIR O' DUNGAREES YOU USETA WEAR ON THE S.S. ANNIE ANANIAS—30 YEARS AGO?
SURE! I JUST CAN'T PART WITH 'EM, YOU KNOW ME, MATEY!! I'M SENTIMENTAL!
(CHUCKLE!! A WORSE BUNCH O' LIARS NEVER LIVED. THERE AINT A NICKEL IN THE CROWD!)

(CHUCKLE!!)—I'LL EMBARRASS 'EM!!—) ER—AHEM! WELL, BOYS, JUDGIN' FROM YOUR TALK--YOU'RE ALL MILLIONAIRES.
AYE, GROGGINS—WE ARE.
CALL ME A MOTH-EATEN BUM-IF WE AINT!!

WELL—SEEIN' AS HOW YOU'RE ALL MILLIONAIRES—WHY SHOULD WE HAVE OUR RE-UNION DINNER AT "ONE LIP TILLES" AS USUAL? LET'S ALL DINE AT THE RITZ!! "(CHUCKLE) THAT'LL STOP 'EM!!"

—ER, THE RITZ? BUT—OF COURSE! LET'S GO!
SURE—ITS ME FAVORITE BEANERY!
LET'S SHOVE OFF TO THE RITZ, MATES.
("HOLY SMOKES! WH—WHAT HAVE I STARTED?")

("I MUST GET RID OF THESE BUMS-SOMEHOW") ER, GENTLEMEN--THERE AREN'T ANY MORE TABLES IN THE MAIN DINING-ROOM.
WHO WANTS TO EAT IN THE MAIN DINING ROOM?
WE WANTS A PRIVATE BANQUET HALL, MATE! AND HANG THE EXPENSE!

("—THEY LOOK LIKE BUMS—BUT SOMEHOW THEIR AIR OF ELEGANCE CONVINCES ME!") A PRIVATE BANQUET HALL—THIS WAY, GENTLE-MEN.
"WHAT LIARS!! FIRST THEY CONVINCE THEM-SELVES THEY ARE MILLIONAIRES! NOW THEY'VE CONVINCED THE HEADWAITER. B—BUT WHO'S GONNA PAY FOR THIS?"
TO BE CONTINUED—

THERE ISN'T A NICKEL BETWEEN 'EM BUT THEY REMAIN TRUE SONS OF THE OLD S.S. ANNIE ANANIAS TO THE BITTER END. (TO BE CONTINUED)

THIS BANQUET FOR TEN CAME TO $285.00!! ALL OF YOUR FRIENDS HAVE LEFT--ON ALL SORTS OF PRETEXTS!! ONE OF YOU HAS GOT TO PAY THIS CHECK!! WHICH ONE?
I W-WILL-- OF COURSE!!
OH, NO, GROGGINS-- IT'S SUCH A TRIFLE-- PERMIT ME!!

("--THIS IS MY CHANCE TO PULL A FAST ONE AND ESCAPE--") OKAY!!-- I'LL PERMIT YOU!!
YOU W-WILL?

GREAT SCOTT!! IT'S HIM!! MY SON!! MY SON!!

IT'S MY LONG LOST BOY!! I AIN'T SEEN THE KID IN 40 YEARS!! HERE, GROGGINS-- TAKE MY WALLET--PAY THE CHECK AND KEEP WHAT'S LEFT!

MY SON! MY SON!

(C-CHOKE!!) I'M IN A TERRIBLE JAM BUT I'VE GOTTA ADMIT THAT WAS SMOOTH --MM-- THIS WALLET IS WELL FILLED---

WELL-FILLED IS KEERECT!! EIGHT OUT-OF-DATE PAWN TICKETS-- TWO POSTERS OFFERIN' A REWARD FOR HIS CAPTURE --DEAD OR ALIVE-- AND A PUNCHED-OUT MEAL TICKET FOR "BELLYACHE BENNY'S"
WELL?

GATHERED OUTSIDE THE RITZ ARE SYMPATHETIC OLD EX-SHIPMATES--
WE'RE ALL SAFELY OUT OF IT--ALL EXCEPT OLD GROGGINS
I'VE NEVER SEEN A BIGGER, TOUGHER HEAD-WAITER!! POOR OLD GROGGINS!!!
I HAVE THE GREATEST CONFIDENCE IN BATHLESS! AFTER ALL, HE SAILED ON THE S.S. ANNIE ANANIAS-- WITH US--HE'LL GET OUT OF IT SOME-HOW
KEERECT-- BUT-- HOW?
SEE NEXT WEEK...

POP HAS BEEN LEFT INSIDE THE RITZ WITH THE $285 BANQUET CHECK---
WE ALL TALKED OUR WAY OUT OF IT, ALL BUT GROGGINS
IF GROGGINS CAN TALK HIS WAY OUT OF THIS--HE DESERVES TO BE MADE PRESIDENT OF THE S.S. ANNIE ANANIAS CLUB
I DOUBT IF HE CAN. WE'VE USED EVERY LIE, DODGE AND GAG KNOWN TO MAN. HE'LL JUST HAVE TO TAKE HIS MEDICINE
GROGGINS IS A DEAD DUCK!

ALL YOUR PALS LEFT ON DIFFERENT PRETEXTS, NOW-- YOU'RE GOING TO PAY THIS CHECK OR--
PAY THE CHECK? OF COURSE!!-- $285, IS IT NOT?

EXACTLY!!
LEGGO O' MY ARM, GOOD-TIME CHARLEY!!

I APPEAL TO YOU, BUB!! MAKE GOOD-TIME CHARLEY LEGGO O' MY ARM!! AND TELL HIM HE CAN'T PAY THE CHECK!! TELL HIM YOU WON'T ACCEPT HIS MONEY
LET GO OF HIS ARM!! I WON'T ACCEPT YOUR MONEY-- ER-- (GULP!!) HEY!! WHAT AM I SAYING?

WHAT IS THIS? I DON'T SEE ANYONE HOLDING YOUR ARM!
YOU DON'T? DID YOU HEAR WHAT HE SAID, CHARLEY?--HE CAN'T SEE YOU! HE CAN SEE ME, CHARLEY--BUT HE CAN'T SEE YOU!! THE POOR LAD IS HALF BLIND, CHARLEY!!

I'M HALF BLIND!!
TAKE IT EASY, BUB--IT'S PROBABLY JUST TEMPORARY SNOWBLINDNESS FROM STARING AT TOO MANY WHITE TABLECLOTHS!!--- SIT DOWN!

THERE NOW, BUB--THAT'LL REST YOUR EYES!! YOU STAY HERE AND TAKE CARE O' HIM, CHARLEY, WHILE I DASHES OUT AND GETS A DOCTOR !!!
8-2

TO OUR NEW PRESIDENT!
LATER--AT BELLYACHE BENNY'S

IT'S MIGHTY FINE O' YOU TO STICK BY ME, CHARLEY-- MIGHTY FINE-- MIGHTY FINE !!
R. VAN BUREN

Abbie an' Slats
Featuring BATHLESS GROGGINS
by RAEBURN VAN BUREN
IF I DIDN'T SEE IT (GASP) WITH ME OWN EYES, I'D NEVER BELIEVE IT! HIM COMIN' BACK T' CAUSE RACK AN' RUIN LIKE—
—LIKE HE DID NEAR FORTY YEARS AGO, WHEN HE SINGLE-HANDED RIPPED UP THE BAR, AN' CAUSED DAMAGE THAT TOOK YEARS T' REPAIR!
CRASH!

HE AIN'T AGED A DAY, NOR IS THE POWER IN HIS FISTS ANY LESS---

I USED TO HEAR MY GRANDMOTHER GASP ABOUT A RED-HAIRED SAILOR WHO FOUGHT LIKE A DEMON, AND MADE LOVE LIKE NO OTHER MAN—
BUT THAT WAS MANY, MANY YEARS AGO—AND YOU—

YOU LOOK NO OLDER THAN US!
TIMES IS FUNNY, GIRLS---

--SOME GETS OLDER, AND SOME (CHUCKLE) HAS LEARNT WAYS NOT TO GET OLDER!

IT'S (SHUDDER) HIM—THE UN-WASHED ONE WITH THE MYSTERIOUS POWER THAT CAN MELT THE COLDEST HEART O' THE COLDEST FEMALE THIS SIDE O' MANDALAY!

IF HALF OF WHAT MY GRANDMOTHER TOLD ME ABOUT THAT RED-HAIRED SAILOR IS TRUE, THEN I'M ABOUT TO DISCOVER LIFE — THE EXCITING WAY!!
YOU'RE MY BEST FRIEND, BUT YOU'LL HAVE TO CLAW YOUR WAY THROUGH ME TO GET TO (SIGH) HIM!
R. VAN BUREN

MEANWHILE---BACK IN CRABTREE CORNERS--- CAN THIS BE POSSIBLE?
2-28
Tm. Reg. U. S. Pat Off.—All rights reserved
Copr. 1960 by United Feature Syndicate, Inc.
MAYBE YES---MAYBE NO. MORE NEXT WEEK

EVEN IN THIS AGE OF ELECTRONIC MIRACLES IT'S HARD TO EXPLAIN HOW ONE BATHLESS GROGGINS IS TAKING LIFE EASY IN CRABTREE CORNERS — WHILE ANOTHER BATHLESS IS SETTING SINGAPORE ON ITS EAR!
CRABTREE CORNERS COURIER

MORE COFFEE, SUE, HONEY, PLEASE!

THE TIP WAS RIGHT. HERE HE COMES NOW — A THROWBACK TO CAPTAIN KIDD! THIS IS THE CHARACTER THAT'S CLEANED OUT MORE SALOONS THAN CARRY NATION!
BOSS CABLED TO GET PICTURES AND STORY ON HIM OR ELSE!

YOU COULD WIND UP ON THE COVER OF THE WORLD'S GREATEST PICTURE MAGAZINE — LOOP!!

ONE WEEK LATER...
IT'S (GASP) ME!! GIVE OR TAKE A COUPLA YEARS AND RED HAIR! IT'S THE SAME BLARSTED FACE I BEEN FEEDIN' FOR MORE'N SIXTY YEARS!
R. VAN BUREN

I GOT TO PERFECT MY REPUTATION, GIRLS. THERE'S NO TELLIN' WHAT THAT IMPOSTOR'S GOIN' TER PULL NEXT!

WHAT'S THAT PECULIAR ODOR COMING FROM THE BAGGAGE ROOM, STEWARDESS?
AT FIRST I THOUGHT IT WAS SOMETHING IN THE LUGGAGE, SIR, BUT--
Tm. Reg. U. S. Pat Off.—All rights reserved
Copr. 1960 by United Feature Syndicate, Inc.

--IT TURNED OUT TO BE--
ME, BUSTER! THE FIRST AIR-BORNE STOWAWAY IN HISTORY! AND THROWIN' ME OVERBOARD'D BE PLAIN MURDER --- WHICH, I UNDERSTANDS, IS CONTRARY TO YER COMPANY'S POLICY!
3-6
TO BE CONTINUED ---

IS THIS THE JOINT WHERE A RED-HAIRED SAILOR'S BEEN CLEANIN' UP ON THEM WHICH QUESTIONS HIS CLAIM THAT HE'S THE TOUGHEST HOMBRE THIS SIDE O' THE CAPE O' GOOD HOPE?
I AM (SOB) LIVIN', BLEEDIN' PROOF DAT HIS CLAIM AIN'T T' BE ARGUED WITH!

AND ME LAST CONSCIOUS WORDS T' YOU, BUSTER, IS — DON'T (GROAN) TANGLE WID HIM!!

STAND UP AND TAKE YER POSITION, YOU BLASTED IMPOSTOR!
ANSWER ME CAREFUL, YOU OLD COOT! YER NAME IS J. PIERPONT GROGGINS AND YER THE CROOKEDEST, ORNERIEST, LYIN'EST, LOVIN'EST SAILOR WHAT EVER FORGED ABLE SEAMAN'S PAPERS?

FLATTERY'LL GET YOU NOWHERE, BUSTER. UP WITH THE DUKES!

THEN YOU ARE HIM!
STOP STALLIN', YOU LILY LIVERED COWARD, AND UP WITH THE DUKES WHO'S HIM?

UNCLE BATHLESS! DON'T YOU (SOB) RECOGNIZE YER OWN FLESH AN' BLOOD — YER YOUNGER BROTHER AVERILL'S BOY, JUNIOR!?
(GASP) JUNIOR!
Tm. Reg. U. S. Pat Off.—All rights reserved
Copr. 1960 by United Feature Syndicate, Inc.

YER OLD MAN WAS THE SPITTIN' IMAGE O' ME — AND YER THE SAME TO HIM!
ALL MY LIFE YOU'VE BEEN MY IDEAL, UNCLE BATHLESS, AND NOW — NOW I ACTUALLY GET TO SEE YOU IN THE FLESH!

THERE AIN'T NOTHIN' ABOUT ME THAT AIN'T EXACTLY LIKE MY OLD MAN TELLS ME YOU WAS, UNCLE BATHLESS — EXCEPT (CHOKE) ONE THING!
WE'RE MOSTLY AS ALIKE AS TWO PEAS IN A POD, NEPHEW — SO WHAT'S ONE LITTLE THING GOIN' TO MATTER? JUST OUT O' CURIOSITY JUNIOR — WHAT IS THE ONE LITTLE THING?
R. VAN BUREN 3-13
YOU'LL SOON (SOB) FIND OUT, BATHLESS!
CONTINUED NEXT WEEK

WHAT'S THE (CHUCKLE) ONE TEENSY LITTLE THING THAT PREVENTS YOU AN' ME FROM BEIN' ALIKE AS TWO PEAS IN A POD, NEPHEW?
YOU PROMISE YOU WON'T BE MAD AT ME, UNCLE BATHLESS?

AFTER ALL, JUNIOR --

--BLOOD IS THICKER 'N WATER!
THAT'S IT, UNCLE BATHLESS!

IT IS?
O' COURSE, UNCLE—WATER! YOU GOT THE REPUTATION — RICHLY DESERVED, I FIGGERS—THAT YOU AND WATER IS WORSE ENEMIES THAN THE HATFIELDS WAS WITH THE McCOYS —

WORSE, BUT GO ON WITH YER STORY, NEPHEW---
WELL, I GOT TO CONFESS TO A WEAKNESS, UNCLE BATHLESS-I---I (SOB) ACTUALLY LIKE TO TAKE BATHS!

FER A MINUTE I THOUGHT IT WAS GONNA BE PEACEFUL AROUND HERE AGAIN!
IT SOUNDS (SHUDDER) WORSE 'N EVER! LIKE HUMAN BONES BEIN' SNAPPED!
CRASH!

W-WHAT HAPPENED INSIDE THERE, BUDDY?
TWO FACTS WAS LEARNED, PAL. FIRST, JUNIOR STILL AIN'T THE TOUGHEST MAN THIS SIDE O' THE CAPE O' GOOD HOPE — AND NEXT---
Tm. Reg. U. S. Pat Off.—All rights reserved
Copr. 1960 by United Feature Syndicate, Inc.

WATER APPLIED TO YER BLARSTED BODY HAS A WEAKENIN' EFFECT.!! CHECK THEM DETAILS WITH ME NEPHEW, AS SOON AS HE REGAINS CONSCIOUSNESS!
R. VAN BUREN
3-20

W-WHAT HAPPENED?
YOU CAME IN SECOND, JUNIOR!!

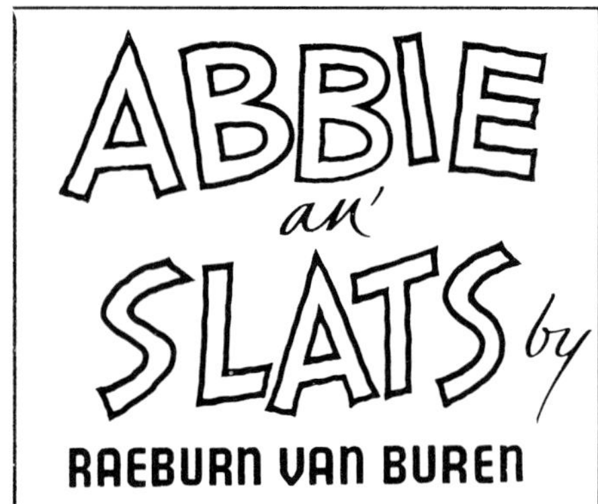
ABBIE an' SLATS by
RAEBURN VAN BUREN

IN A FEW MINUTES, HAGGIS--IT'LL BE ALL COOLED AND FINISHED!!! THE RESULTS OF MONTHS OF HARD WORK--BUT LOOK WHAT WE HAVE---A PERMANENT GLUE!!!!
AYE, BATHLESS!! THE ONE GLUE WHICH NEVER LETS GO!!! ONCE ONE OBJECT IS GLUED TO ANOTHER WITH OUR GLUE---- THEY STAY GLUED FOREVER!!!

KEERECT!! YOU'VE BEEN A GREAT OLD MATE TO WORK WITH, HAGGIS--- ALWAYS PATIENT, ALWAYS CHEERFUL, ALWAYS UNDERSTANDIN'----
AYE!!! AND YOU, BATHLESS!!! AH--- WHAT A MON YOU'VE BEEN TO WORK WITH IN THIS GR-REAT SCIENTIFIC EXPERIMENT!!! A MON IN A MILLION!!! ALWAYS BY MY SIDE--- BE IT FAIR WEATHER OR FOUL!!!

KEERECT, HAGGIS--- AND I'LL ALWAYS STAY AT YOUR SIDE. PUT IT THERE, PAL!!
NOBODY I'D RATHER HAVE AT MY SIDE, MON!!! SHAKE!!

Copr. 1941 by United Feature Syndicate, Inc.
Tm. Reg. U. S. Pat. Off.—All rights reserved

OUCH!! YA BLASTED SEA APE--LOOK WHAT YA DONE!!!
T'WAS YOU THAT DONE IT---YE GOAT-FACED AULD BABOON!!
SPLUT!

LEGGO O'ME!!
I CAN'T LET GO O' YE!!

THAT'S K-KEERECT--- YOU C-CAN'T!!! W-WHAT WAS IT YOU WERE JUST SAYING ABOUT G-GLUE----?
ONCE ONE OBJECT IS GLUED TO ANOTHER OBJECT WITH OUR GLUE THEY STAYS GLUED!!!

AND I W-WAS JUST SAYIN'---I'D ALWAYS BE AT YOUR S-SIDE, HAGGIS!! OH--HOW KEERECT I WAS--- HOW HORRIBLY KEERECT!!
AYE!! THIS MAY DEVELOP INTO A CONFUSIN' SITUATION, AULD MON!!!
HOW TRUE!!! HOW HORRIBLY TRUE!----- ----TO BE CONTINUED-----
DEC-28

Copr. 1942 by United Feature Syndicate, Inc.
Tm. Reg. U.S. Pat. Off.—All rights reserved

OUR BARGAIN IS AS FOLLOWS: WE'VE BOTH GOT SECRET DATES AND BY A PECULIAR COINCIDENCE, WE'VE BOTH GOT DATES WITH FASCINATIN' WIDDERS
AYE-- AND BY ANOTHER REMARKABLE COINCIDENCE-- BOTH OUR WIDDERS HAVE JEALOUS ADMIRERS AND HAVE MADE US BOTH PROMISE NOT TO REVEAL THE IDENTITY OF OUR WIDDERS TO ANYONE IN THE WORLD-- WHICH WOULD INCLUDE OURSELVES

KEERECT!! NOW--- YOUR DATE IS FROM 8 TO 10. MINE FROM 10 TO 12. SO I CHLOROFORMS MYSELF FOR TWO HOURS --- YOU KEEPS YOUR DATE-- THEN YOU CHLOROFORMS YOURSELF FOR TWO HOURS AND I KEEP MY DATE
AYE!! SO THOT WHEN THE WHOLE ROMONTIC EVENIN' IS OVER-- NEITHER ONE OF US WILL HAVE SEEN THE OTHER ONE'S WIDDER-- THUS PRESERVIN' THE SECRECY DESIRED BY BOTH OUR FAIR LADIES!!!

LATER---
HE'S SLEEPING LIKE A BABY!!! AND NOW TO VISIT MY FASCINATIN' WIDDER!

HAGGIS!! YOU PROMISED NEVER TO LET ANYONE KNOW YOU WERE CALLING ON ME!! YOU KNOW I HAVE A CERTAIN INSANELY JEALOUS ADMIRER-- AND THIS FRIEND OF YOURS--- MIGHT TALK!!
HE WON'T TALK, BEULAH!
AND I HAD TO BRING HIM. WE'RE ACCIDENTALLY GLUED TOGETHER WITH THE PERFECT GLUE-- IT WON'T EVER COME APART!!! WE'RE SIAMESE TWINS IN A WAY-- BUT-- HE'S UNCONSCIOUS-- SEE?

(---MERCY!!--IT'S HIM-- BATHLESS GROGGINS--- THE JEALOUS ONE!!")
ARE YOU S-SURE--- HE'S WELL CHLOROFORMED?
AYE!! WE'LL BE AS ALONE AS IF WE WERE ON A DESERT ISLAND FOR ABOUT TWO HOURS!

LATER---
IT'S N-NEARLY T-TEN O'CLOCK--THOSE TWO HOURS ARE NEARLY UP. H-HADN'T YOU BETTER G-GO NOW?
AH, BEULAH, MY SWEET--I HATE TO LEAVE YE TONIGHT. TONIGHT YE SEEM MORE BEAUTIFUL THAN EVER--- YOUR FACE IS FLUSHED--AND YE SEEM TO BE TREMBLIN' WITH EMOTION AS YE HOLD MY HAND!!

W-WHERE AM I?--AH YES--- I REMEMBER!!! HEY--- IS IT TEN O'CLOCK YET?
JUST ABOUT. I'VE ALREADY TAKEN MY DOSE O'CHLOROFORM. I'M PASSIN' OUT NOW IN FACT--- G-G-GOODBYE, BATH--LESS--S-----

"I ONLY TOOK HALF A DOSE!! I'LL COME TO IN AN HOUR-- BUT I WON'T LET ON. I'VE ALWAYS WONDERED WHETHER HIS LOVE-MAKING TECHNIQUE WAS AS SNAPPY AS HE CLAIMS IT IS-- AND NOW I'LL BE THERE TO SEE!!
HE'S SLEEPIN' LIKE A LAMB AND NOW--- TO MY BEULAH!!

ONE HOUR LATER----
AH, BEULAH, MY SWEET--- I SEEM TO THRILL YOU MORE TONIGHT THAN EVER BEFORE IN THE COURSE O'OUR GREAT ROMANCE---YOU'RE TREMBLIN'
("--TREMBLING, MY EYE. I'VE GOT THE SHAKES!! OF ALL THE PEOPLE IN THE WORLD---WHY DID THESE TWO HAVE TO GET GLUED TOGETHER!!!")

YE DOOBLE-CROSSING SCOUNDREL!!!
TO BE VIOLENTLY CONTINUED--- NEXT WEEK

SO!!! YE DOOBLE CROSSING SCOONDREL!! IT WAS MY OWN BEULAH YE WERE COURTIN'-- WHILE YE THOUGHT I HAD TAKEN ENOUGH CHLOROFORM TO KEEP ME UNCONSCIOUS FOR TWO HOURS!!!-- WELL--I ONLY TOOK ENOUGH TO PUT ME OUT FOR AN HOUR--- I CHEATED ON THE CHLOROFORM, YE DOOBLE CROSSER!!!
HA!
1-18

SMASH !!!

KLUNK !!

I'LL PROP THIS SNAKE UP AGAINST THIS SECOND STORY WINDOW---AND THEN I'LL SMASH HIM CLEAR OUT OF IT !!!

SMASH !!!
OOPS!! I DINNA FIGURE ON THIS !!
Copr. 1942 by United Feature Syndicate, Inc.
Tm. Reg. U. S. Pat. Off.—All rights reserved

WE'RE APART !!! AT LAST I'M FREE OF YOU--- YOU TREACHEROUS RAT !!
I'M THANKFUL T'BE RID O'YE, YE UGLY OLD SEA-SERPENT !!! I NEVER WANT TO SEE YE AGAIN !! NEVER!

ME NEITHER---!!!! I'M FREE OF YE AND--- ???--SAY-- WE DID COME APART AT THAT--- HMMM--- THEN THE PERFECT GLUE WE INVENTED WASN'T SO PERFECT AFTER ALL
THAT'S RIGHT!!! HMMM--MAYBE WE DINNA PUT ENOUGH MIXTURE "A" IN IT---

PERHAPS---BUT ON THE OTHER HAND-- MAYBE WE PUT TOO MUCH MIXTURE "B" IN IT---
PERHAPS A DASH O'VIT-AMIN "O" MIGHT HAVE GIVEN IT THAT PERMA-NENT QUALITY---

WE'LL TRY BOTH THEM IDEAS RIGHT NOW. YOU AND ME--- WE'LL WORK ON THAT GLUE UNTIL IT IS PERFECT!! I'LL NEVER LEAVE YOUR SIDE UNTIL THE JOB IS DONE
AYE, BATHLESS-- AND I'LL STICK WITH YOU--- TO THE END!
R. VAN BUREN

# ABBIE an' SLATS



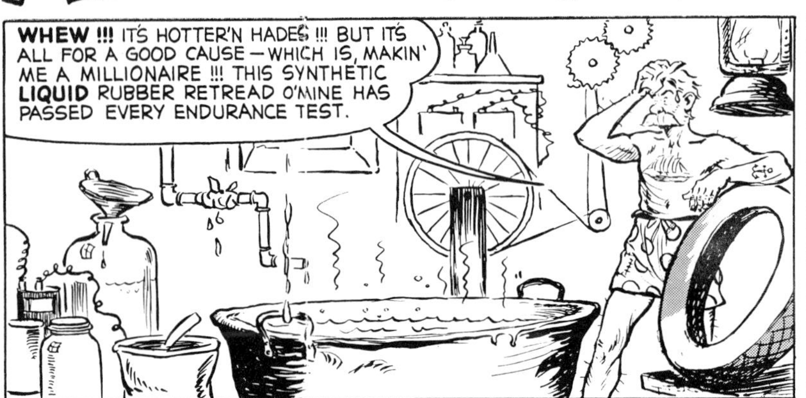

CONTINUED FROM LAST WEEK
THERE'S SOMETHIN' AWFUL PECULIAR ABOUT YOU, BATHLESS !!! BENNY JUST ACCIDENTALLY WHACK-ED YOU SO HARD WITH THAT CUE STICK IT WOULD OF CUT AN ORDINARY MAN IN HALF !!!
BUT YOU DIDN'T SEEM TO FEEL IT!!!
I DIDN'T FEEL IT !!

HMM—I'M JUST BEGINNIN' T'GET AN INKLIN' O' WHAT'S SO PECULIAR ABOUT ME—BUT I WON'T BELIEVE IT UNTIL I GIVES IT THE ACID TEST !!

THE ACID TEST BEIN' "FEET" McFLOOGLE !!!—THE MEANEST PRACTICAL JOKER IN TOWN
*Copr. 1942 by United Feature Syndicate, Inc.
Tm. Reg. U. S. Pat. Off.—All rights reserved

I'LL STICK MY CHIN OUT—
DRY GOO
NO TIC

I'VE WAITED FIVE MINUTES FOR "FEET" TO TAKE ADVANTAGE O' MY POSITION IN HIS USUAL HUMOROUS WAY—???
GR-R-ROAN !!!

(GROAN !!!)THERE'S SOME-THIN' WRONG WITH YOU-YOU AIN'T HUMAN !!! OHHH !!! I THINK I'VE BUSTED MY TOES ON YOU !!!

Y-YOU KICKED ME, HUH, "FEET"?
(GROANNNN !!!) FOUR TIMES !!!!—OH, MY TOES, MY TOES !!!

THANK YOU,"FEET"—THANK YOU, PAL !!!!

NOW I KNOW !!!! THAT LIQUID RETREAD I INVENTED FOR AUTO TIRES—THAT STUFF I FELL INTO —WORKS JUST THE SAME ON HUMAN SKIN !!!! I'M RE-TREADED !!! I'M IMMUNE TO PAIN !!! NOTHIN' CAN HURT ME !!
(9-6)

AND NOTHIN' CAN REMOVE MY RETREAD JOB—EXCEPT SOAP AN' WATER !!! WHICH MEANS THAT ON ME—IT'S PERMANENT !!!
A HUMAN RETREAD JOB !!! IT OPENS A WORLD OF POSSIBILITIES TO POP !!!
(TO BE CONTINUED)

I'M A MIRACLE MAN !!! I'M RETREADED !! BY THE SHEEREST ACCIDENT I FLOPPED IN-TO A TUB O' SYNTHETIC LIQUID RUBBER I IN-VENTED-- WHICH LEFT A THIN COLORLESS COVERIN' ALL OVER ME—MAKIN' ME IM-MUNE TO PAIN—

AN' NOTHIN' CAN REMOVE IT EXCEPT SOAP AN' WATER— WHICH MEANS THAT ON ME IT'S PERMANENT !! THERE'S JUST ONE WAY TO MAKE THIS PAY OFF—I'LL BECOME CHAMPION OF THE WORLD, MAKE A MILLION AND RETIRE UN-DEFEATED !!

BIG MIKE JONES FIGHT MANAGER AND PROMOTER

I'D LIKE TO TANGLE WITH THE CHAMP, BUT I REALIZE THAT I'VE GOTTA POLISH OFF A FEW TOUGH PUNKS FIRST. MATCH ME WITH A HALF DOZEN OF 'EM, BUB —I'LL TAKE 'EM ALL ON IN A WEEK AND LICK THE CHAMP THE WEEK AFTER THAT.
("IT'S PITIFUL HOW OLD AGE AFFECTS THE BRAIN. I'LL BRUSH HIM OFF KIND-LY—LIKE")

YOU'RE A SWEET OLD FELLA, GRANDPAW, BUT PLEASE SCRAM BEFORE YOU FALLS APART FROM SENILITY RIGHT HERE IN MY NICE NEAT OFFICE
DO YOU THINK I'LL HAVE TO LICK AS MANY AS SIX CON-TENDERS BE-FORE I GETS TO THE CHAMP? WOULDN'T THREE OF THE TOUGHEST DO— IF I LICKED 'EM ALL THE SAME NIGHT ?

TOSS HIM OUT ON HIS EAR, KNUCKLES
I HATES TO DO THIS, OUTA RE-SPECT FOR YOUR AGE, SIR—BUT YOUSE IS ANNOYIN' THE BOSS—
SOCK!!

LOOK, BOSS—HE'S STILL STANDIN'—
HIT HIM AGAIN, KNUCKLES —THIS IS INTERESTIN'-
YOU AIN'T SEEN NOTHIN' YET. DO LIKE THE BOSS SAYS, KNUCKLES, AND DON'T SPARE THE HORSES !

HE'S STILL STANDIN' !!! THAT'S A SCIENTIFIC MIRACLE ! I'LL GIVE OUT WITH ONE MYSELF-STRICTLY IN THE INTERESTS O' SCIENCE
CRRACKKK !!!

DON'T, BOSS, DON'T !!! IT'S LIKE BOUNCIN' YOUR FISTS OFF A STONE WALL !!!
OUCH !!! MY KNUCKLES !!
SLAM !!!

SIGN THERE PAL— (GROANNN !!!)—OH— (GROANNN !!!)—THIS IS THE LUCKIEST DAY O' MY—GROANN! —LIFE !!
R. VAN BUREN
(9-13)
TO BE CONTINUED---

COMEDY ACT SCHEDULED AS SEMI-FINAL TONIGHT.
WHAT PROMISES TO BE HILARIOUS ENTERTAINMENT FOR BOXING FANS TONIGHT IS THE 15-ROUND SEMI-FINAL WHICH MATCHES "TOUGH TOBY" WITH THAT BEWHISKERED METHUSELAH, BATTLING GROGGINS. GROGGINS, AN OLD WAR HORSE DATING BACK TO THE DAYS OF "WILD" DONOVAN —
BATTLING GROGGINS
OLD GROGGINS IS AN ANCIENT MARINER WHO FANCIES HIMSELF AS A FIGHTER AT AN AGE WHEN MOST MEN ARE CONTENT TO DROOL BY THEIR FIREPLACES. "TOUGH TOBY" PROMISES TO PUT THE VENERABLE GROGGINS OUT OF HIS MISERY QUICKLY TONIGHT. "I'LL DO IT WITH ONE PUNCH," SAID TOUGH TOBY "OR LESS".
TOUGH TOBY
TOUGH TOBY COLLAPSES IN FIFTEENTH ROUND
GROGGINS AWARDED DECISION WHEN OPPONENT KEELS OVER FROM EXHAUSTION AFTER HAVING POUNDED GROGGINS UNMERCIFULLY FOR THE WHOLE ROUTE.



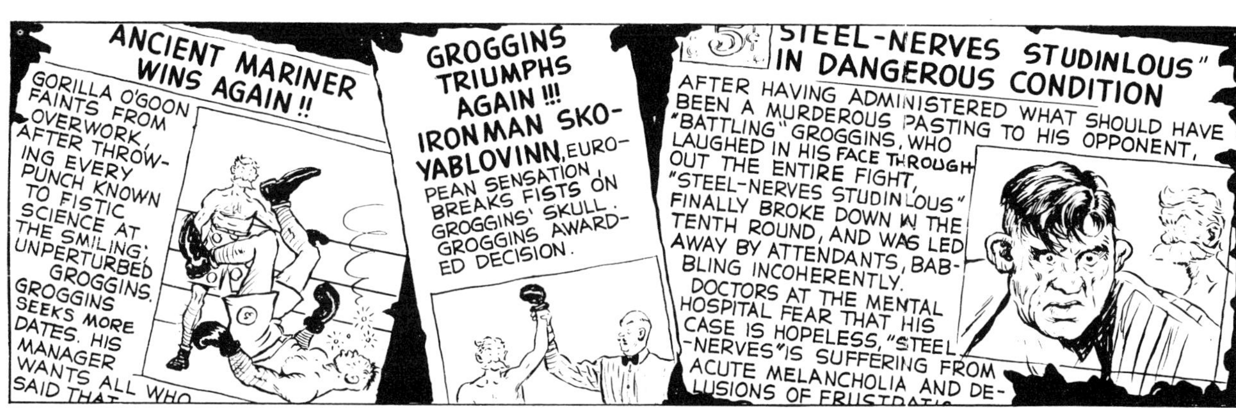
ANCIENT MARINER WINS AGAIN !!
GORILLA O'GOON FAINTS FROM OVERWORK AFTER THROWING EVERY PUNCH KNOWN TO FISTIC SCIENCE AT THE SMILING, UNPERTURBED GROGGINS. GROGGINS SEEKS MORE DATES. HIS MANAGER WANTS ALL WHO SAID THAT —
GROGGINS TRIUMPHS AGAIN !!!
IRONMAN SKO-YABLOVINN, EUROPEAN SENSATION, BREAKS FISTS ON GROGGINS' SKULL. GROGGINS AWARDED DECISION.
5¢
"STEEL-NERVES STUDINLOUS" IN DANGEROUS CONDITION
AFTER HAVING ADMINISTERED WHAT SHOULD HAVE BEEN A MURDEROUS PASTING TO HIS OPPONENT, "BATTLING" GROGGINS, WHO LAUGHED IN HIS FACE THROUGHOUT THE ENTIRE FIGHT, "STEEL-NERVES STUDINLOUS" FINALLY BROKE DOWN IN THE TENTH ROUND, AND WAS LED AWAY BY ATTENDANTS, BABBLING INCOHERENTLY.
DOCTORS AT THE MENTAL HOSPITAL FEAR THAT HIS CASE IS HOPELESS. "STEEL-NERVES" IS SUFFERING FROM ACUTE MELANCHOLIA AND DELUSIONS OF FRUSTRATION.

FANS DEMAND THAT CHAMP FIGHT GROGGINS !!!
CHAMP FORCED BY PUBLIC CLAMOR TO SIGN FOR BOUT WITH BATTLI—

IN CHAMP'S CAMP
FOR DE FOIST TIME IN MY CAREER, I'M NOIVUSS, GHOULASHIHAN !!! DAT OLD GUY I GOTTA FIGHT IS OUT OF DIS WORLD !!! ACCORDIN' TO TH' MEDICAL REPORTS HE'S A WRECK !!! HE'S GOT NO GOOD HABITS, HE'S LED A LIFE THAT WOULDA KILLED TEN ORDINARY MEN—
R. Van Buren

HE DON'T TRAIN, HE DON'T LIVE RIGHT, HE LOOKS LIKE SOMETHIN' THE CAT DRAGGED IN—AN' YET NOBODY KIN LICK HIM !!! IT'S GOT ME NOIVUSS !!
HMM—THERE'S SOMETHING PECULIAR ABOUT THAT OLD GUY—
(9-20)

ALL THAT POWER O' HIS—IT AIN'T NATURAL !! HE MUST HAVE SOME SERET SOURCE O' STREN'TH NOBODY KNOWS ABOUT—AN' WE GOTTA FIND OUT WHAT IT IS !

A FEW HOURS LATER.
DID YOU SEND FOR ME, BUB ?
RIGHT. SIT DOWN. I'VE GOT A JOB FOR YOU—DELILAH !!!
TO BE CONTINUED ---

THE OFFICE OF DAN GHOULASHIHAN, MANAGER OF THE WORLD'S CHAMPION.
WHAT'S THE ANGLE THIS TIME, BUB?
HA!! HA!! NEVER STRUCK ME BEFORE HOW APPROPRIATE IT IS YOUR NAME IS DELILAH!!

DELILAH, YOUR JOB IS WITH A SAMSON!! THE CHAMP, YOU KNOW, IS SCHEDULED TO TANGLE WITH "BATTLING" GROGGINS TOMORROW NIGHT.
YEAH. THAT'S THE OLD GOAT THEY CALL "THE ANCIENT MARINER"—THE ONE THEY ARE ALL TALKIN' ABOUT. THE ONE NOBODY CAN LICK.

RIGHT!!! NOW, THE WAY I FIGURE IT—IT ISN'T NATURAL FOR AN OLD WRECK LIKE THAT., WITH THE HABITS HE HAS, LIVIN' THE KIND OF LIFE HE'S LED, TO HAVE THE STRENGTH HE SEEMS TO HAVE. IT ISN'T NATURAL, I TELL YOU!! HE'S GOT SOME SECRET SOURCE O' STRENGTH, I'M POSITIVE!

BEFORE TOMORROW NIGHT, YOU'VE GOT TO FIND OUT JUST WHAT THAT SENILE SAMSON'S SECRET SOURCE OF STRENGTH IS—AND CLIP HIM, DELILAH, CLIP HIM!! HE SPENDS ALL HIS TIME SUNNING HIMSELF AT THE BEACH. HE'S PROBABLY THERE NOW
I'M OFF, BUB.

OH—I'M SORRY!! I HOPE I DIDN'T HURT YOU!!!
HURT ME—THE NEXT CHAMPION OF THE WORLD? DON'T BE SILLY, M'AM!!

I THOUGHT YOU LOOKED FAMILIAR!!! YOU'RE "BATTLING" GROGGINS. YOU'RE MUCH HANDSOMER THAN YOUR PICTURES
KEERECT!!

OH—IT'S SO THRILLING TO MEET CELEBRITIES!! COME ON, LET'S GO INTO THE WATER!!
ME—GO INTO THAT—(UGH!!) WATER? NO M'AM!! I NEVER TOUCHES THE BLARSTED STUFF INTERNALLY OR EXTERNALLY

(—"HMM—I MAY BE CRAZY—BUT MAYBE WATER IS THE CLUE. I'LL GIVE THAT THEORY THE ACID TEST—") HELP!!! I'M DROWNING—HELP!! MR. GROGGINS!
Copr. 1942 by United Feature Syndicate, Inc.
Tm. Reg. U. S. Pat. Off.—All rights reserved

("MY WATER THEORY WAS WRONG")—OH, THANK YOU—(GLUB!!!)—MR. GROGGINS—

THE NAME ISN'T GROGGINS, MISS. I'M WATKINS, THE LIFEGUARD. GOSH—IT WAS LUCKY THAT OLD GEEZER KNEW WHERE TO FIND ME. I'D QUIT FOR THE DAY—AND HE WAS THE ONLY PERSON ON THE BEACH. PERSONALLY I THINK HE WOULD HAVE LET YOU DROWN RATHER THAN GO INTO THE WATER HIMSELF!!!

I NEVER SAW SUCH AN EXPRESSION OF FEAR AND LOATHING AS I SAW ON THAT OLD GEEZER'S FACE WHEN HE WATCHED ME DIVE INTO THE WATER. HE WOULDN'T STEP NEARER THEN TEN YARDS FROM THE EDGE.
(—"THAT WAS THE ACID TEST! MY WATER THEORY WAS RIGHT. SAMSON!! HERE COMES YOUR DELILAH!!
(9-27)
TO BE CONTINUED—

BATTLING GROGGINS MEETS CHAMP TO-NIGHT !!! "ANCIENT MARINER" CONFIDENT HE WILL WIN AGAIN !!!
AND WHY SHOULDN'T I BE CONFIDENT !!! I'M RETREADED !!! NOTHIN' CAN HURT ME !!! I FEELS NO PAIN !!! AND THE RETREAD WON'T COME OFF UNLESS I COMES INTO CONTACT WITH WATER—AND THERE'S SMALL FEAR O' THAT !!!

SWEETS !!! I WANTED TO DRINK A LAST TOAST WITH YOU BE-FORE THE FIGHT—TO VICTORY !!

OKAY, HERBIE—DO YOUR STUFF
RIGHT, DELILAH !!!
GLOOP !!!

I'M SURE MY THEORY IS RIGHT—THAT HIS FEAR OF WATER IS DUE TO THE FACT THAT HE KNOWS THAT—SOMEHOW—IT'LL WEAKEN HIM !!! THOSE KNOCKOUT POWDERS WILL WEAR OFF IN AN HOUR—JUST IN TIME FOR THE FIGHT.

AN HOUR LATER
WAKE-UP, BATTLER—THE FIGHT'S ON !!!
LET'S GO !!!

WHAT AN IMAGINATION I'VE GOT !!! I THOUGHT I FELT THAT ONE !!! BUT, OF COURSE—THAT'S RIDICULOUS—I'M RETREADED !!!

WHAM !!

ONE—TWO—
??? WHERE'S THAT GRAVY SPOT ??? IT'S BEEN ON M' LEFT ARM SINCE CLANCEY'S CLAMBAKE ON LABOR DAY, 1910 !!! IT'S GONE !!!
OCT-4

THREE—FOUR—FIVE—
THERE'S BEEN SOME DIRTY WORK !!! I'M CLEAN !!! I'M NOT RE-TREADED ANY MORE!

—SIX—SEVEN—EIGHT—NINE—
HEY !!! WAIT !!! STOP COUNTIN'—I GIVES UP !!! HE WINS !!!

I'M NO FOOL !!! I KNOW WHEN I'M LICKED !!!
R. VAN BUREN

ABBIE an' SLATS by
RAEBURN VAN BUREN

GUESS I'LL TOSS SOME DARTS—BUT HMMM—THAT BULL'S-EYE IS TOO FAR GONE. MAYBE I CAN DIG SOMETHIN' UP OUTA TH' CELLAR
Copr. 1943 by United Feature Syndicate, Inc.
Tm. Reg. U. S. Pat. Off.—All rights reserved

HA !!

ONE NIGHT, 20 YEARS AGO, IN HAMBURGISTAN, I WAS BROKE AN' HUNGRY ENOUGH TO ACCEPT AN INVITE T' DINNER AT FAT FATIMA'S HOUSE. HOW DID I KNOW IT WAS A CUSTOM O' THE PLACE THAT ANY BACHELOR WHO ACCEPTED A HOME-COOKED DINNER AT A SINGLE DAME'S HOUSE ---
WHAM!

--HAD T' MARRY HER BEFORE HE LEFT? THAT WAS A CLOSE ONE !! SHE SURE WAS FAST ON HER PINS FOR HER WEIGHT!! I BARELY MADE THE BOAT !!

BULL'S-EYE !! WELL, THAT'S ALL PART O' MY PAST—DEAD AN' GONE AN' BETTER LEFT FORGOTTEN
WHAM!

THE SCENE SHIFTS THOUSAND OF MILES, TO THE PROVINCE OF HAMBURGISTAN, IN INDIA–THE PALACE OF THE MAHARAJAH
THIS IS ONE OF THE MAHARAJAH'S LONGEST ROMANCES. HE MARRIED HER 12 MINUTES AGO–AND HE IS STILL NOT TIRED OF LOOKING AT HER
YES, BUT, ALAS–SHE WILL RUIN THE ROMANCE. JUST AS ALL THE OTHERS HAVE IN THE SAME SILLY WAY !! WAIT AND SEE !

OH, SWEET MAHARAJAH !! YOUR EVER-LOVING LITTLE SCHEHEREZADE WOULD SIT ON YOUR UNUTTERABLY SPLENDID LAP
YOU WOULD, EH ? THAT'S ALL !! YOU'RE JUST LIKE ALL THE REST OF THEM ! THE ROMANCE IS OVER ! TAKE HER TO THE HAREM ! AND DON'T LET ME EVER SEE HER AGAIN
THEY ALWAYS MAKE THE SAME MISTAKE
ANOTHER ROYAL MARRIAGE GOES ON THE ROCKS!

WHENEVER A NEW WIFE MAKES SO BOLD AS TO DARE APPROACH THE MAHARAJAH—THAT DOES IT !
ALL THE MAHARAJAH WANTS OF A NEW WIFE IS JUST TO LOOK AT HER. BUT WOMEN CAN'T SEEM TO UNDERSTAND THAT !
8-15

I AM (YAWN) BORED ! AND WHEN I'M BORED I USUALLY TAKE UNTO ME A NEW WIFE. BUT IS THERE A NEW FACE WORTHY OF MY GAZE IN ALL HAMBURGISTAN ?
YES, ADORABLE MAHARAJAH !! A THOUSAND TIMES YES ! I HAVE DISCOVERED THE MOST BEAUTIFUL NEW FACE IN ALL THE WORLD–THE DAUGHTER OF FAT FATIMA !!

THEN (YAWN!) PAY FAT FATIMA ANY MARRIAGE FEE SHE NAMES—AND BRING THE GORGEOUS ONE TO ME!
AH–BUT SWEET MAHARAJAH–THERE ARE GRAVE DIFFICULTIES. FAT FATIMA WAS ONCE BITTERLY DISAPPOINTED IN LOVE
SHE WILL NEVER CONSENT TO HER DAUGHTER'S MARRIAGE EVEN TO YOU–UNTIL SOMEHOW WE ERASE THE MEMORY OF THAT DISAPPOINTMENT !
TO BE CONTINUED.

NEVER ENJOYED THROWIN' DARTS SO MUCH AS SINCE I PUT THAT UP. SHE NEARLY NABBED ME THAT NIGHT.
WHAM!
FAT FATIMA
NOW APPE NIGH AT
ALI BABA
NO COVER CHAR

THE SCENE SHIFTS EAST OF SUEZ. THE PALACE OF THE MAHARAJAH OF HAMBURGISTAN.
(SIGH!!) MY 669 TH MARRIAGE HAS JUST COLLAPSED !! I AM BEGINNING TO LOSE FAITH IN MATRIMONY BUT WHAT ELSE IS THERE TO WHILE AWAY THE TIME TELL ME — IS THERE LEFT A SUFFICIENTLY DELECTABLE UNMARRIED DAMSEL IN ALL HAMBURGISTAN ?
AH, YES, O MAGNIFICENT ONE, THE MOST DELECTABLE OF ALL—THE DAUGHTER OF FAT FATIMA !!

BUT, FAT FATIMA WAS ONCE DISAPPOINTED IN LOVE. BECAUSE OF THAT BITTER MEMORY, SHE WILL NOT CONSENT TO HER DAUGHTER'S MARRIAGE EVEN TO SUCH A DESIRABLE ONE AS YOU, O DESIRABLE ONE
BAH !! EVERYONE HAS HIS PRICE

MY USUAL MARRIAGE FEE TO THE MOTHER IS TWO SWINE, TWO DUCKS AND A CURLY-HAIRED YAK. IN THIS CASE, DOUBLE THE FEE AND BRING BACK THE DAMSEL. I HAVE SPOKEN !! BEGONE, VERMIN !!
TO HEAR IS TO OBEY !

THE DESERT ABODE OF FAT FATIMA...
WITHDRAW FROM SIGHT, DEERVANA, MY SWEET. MEN APPROACH ! LET THEM NOT BEFOUL YOUR BEAUTY WITH THEIR RED-RIMMED BEADY EYES !!
8-22

WE ARE EMISSARIES OF THE MAHARAJAH !! WE BRING GLAD TIDINGS OF INDESCRIBABLE JOY. YOU WILL GET TWICE THE STANDARD CATALOGUE PRICE FOR THE HAND OF YOUR DAUGHTER IN MARRIAGE TO THE MAHARAJAH, O FORTUNATE HAG !
A PLAGUE ON YOU AND YOUR MARRIAGES !

THE VERY WORD MARRIAGE CAUSES ME UNSPEAKABLE ANGUISH ! 20 YEARS AGO I FELL MADLY IN LOVE WITH A FASCINATING RED-BEARDED SAILOR FROM BEYOND THE BLUE HORIZON. HE REJOICED IN THE NAME OF "BATHLESS"
P. VAN BUREN

CASTING ALL MODESTY TO THE WINDS, I INVITED HIM TO DINE WITH ME. BECAUSE HE WAS STARVING AND PENNILESS, HE ACCEPTED
SO, NATURALLY, ACCORDING TO THE SACRED CUSTOM OF OUR COUNTRY, HE MARRIED YOU, NO ?

(SOB !!!) NO !! AND THAT IS PRECISELY WHY I HATE MARRIAGE !! HAVING WOLFED DOWN EVERY MORSEL OF FOOD, HE RAN OFF LIKE A WOUNDED GAZELLE WHEN I ATTEMPTED TO EMBRACE HIM !! I STILL FEEL THE PAIN IN MY HEART !!

LATER, I ENTERED INTO A LOVELESS MARRIAGE WITH ONE ALL-CAT, WHO WAS MYSTERIOUSLY SMOTHERED ON OUR HONEYMOON. THE FRUIT OF THIS UNHAPPY UNION IS MY DAUGHTER DEERVANA ! BUT—SHE WILL NEVER SUFFER AS I HAVE !! TAKE AWAY YOUR GIFTS ! I HATE MARRIAGES !
UNLESS WE CAN FIX UP THAT 20-YEAR-OLD ROMANCE OF HERS— WE WILL NEVER GET DEERVANA FOR OUR MERCIFUL MASTER, THE MAHARAJAH
AND IF WE DON'T OUR MERCIFUL MASTER WILL HAVE US DISEMBOWELED AND TOSSED TO THE CROCODILES. WE MUST FIND THAT BATHLESS
TO BE CONTINUED....

IN THE HALL OF RECORDS.

YOU ARE GROGGINS—THE ONE THEY CALL "BATHLESS," IT IS PLAIN TO SEE
KEERECT!
WE HAVE FOLLOWED YOUR TRAIL FROM ONE POLICE COURT TO ANOTHER IN EVERY PORT IN THE SEVEN SEAS, O GREAT DISTURBER OF THE PEACE, COMMENCING WITH HAMBURGISTAN

HAMBURGISTAN!! WHY, I AIN'T BEEN THERE FOR 20 YEARS—NOT SINCE THE NIGHT I ESCAPED FROM—UGH!—FAT FATIMA!!
THAT IS PRECISELY WHY WE ARE HERE. YOU MUST RETURN TO THE WIDOW, FAT FATIMA, AND WED HER!!
IF YOU DO NOT—WE SHALL (SIGH) JOIN OUR ANCESTORS.

THEN YOU'LL JOIN YOUR ANCESTORS, THAT'S SURE! SO LONG, BOYS!!
HE HAS SPOKEN!
WOE UNTO US!

THE FOLLOWING EVENING!
BE A GOOD FELLER, AND DELIVER THIS PROJECTOR AND FILM TO THE ZOOTNAGLES—IT'S ON YOUR WAY HOME!
KEERECT!
CAMERA SHOP
FILMS DELIVERED 12 HOURS
PHOTO SUPPLIES

KLOP!!
Copr. 1943 by United Feature Syndicate, Inc.
Tm. Reg. U. S. Pat. Off.—All rights reserved

WEEKS LATER---
YOU AIN'T SAID A BLARSTED WORD T'ME SINCE YOU SHANGHAIED ME! WHERE ARE YOU TAKING ME—AN' WHY?
WE ARE TAKING YOU TO HAMBURGISTAN—THAT'S WHERE!
AND YOU WILL WED FAT FATIMA—THAT'S WHY!

SOME TIME AGO THE MAHARAJAH ASSIGNED US TO GAIN THE CONSENT OF THE HAG, FAT FATIMA, TO THE MARRIAGE OF HER DELECTABLE DAUGHTER, DEERVANA, TO THE MAHARAJAH. IF WE FAILED, WE WOULD BE TOSSED TO THE CROCODILES
NATURALLY, WE WERE UPSET WHEN THE WIDOW, FAT FATIMA, REFUSED TO GIVE HER CONSENT. HER LIFE, IT SEEMS, HAD BECOME EMBITTERED BY HER FRUSTRATED LOVE FOR YOU, O BATHLESS ONE
R. VAN BUREN
9-5

ONLY BY BRINGING YOU BACK TO THE STUBBORN, MOROSE CRONE, FAT FATIMA, COULD WE RESTORE HER FAITH IN MEN AND GAIN HER CONSENT TO THE MATCH
ME—MARRY FAT FATIMA? NO!!

NO?
NO!!

NO?
NO, BLARST YOU, NO!!
TO BE CONTINUED--

IN A DUNGEON IN HAMBURGISTAN—EAST OF SUEZ.
YOU WILL WED FAT FATIMA?
NO !!

STILL NO ?
A THOUSAND TIMES NO !!!

WOE IS US !! WE HAVE TRIED EVERY FORM OF TORTURE KNOWN TO MAN—AND STILL HE SAYS NO !!
THERE ARE NO MORE TORTURES LEFT IN THE BOOK. WE ARE (SIGH !!) LICKED !! AS IS THE CUSTOM OF OUR COUNTRY WHEN EVERY TORTURE HAS FAILED WE WILL GIVE HIM THE CEREMONIAL BATH—AND SET HIM FREE

CHOKE !!

ALL RIGHT !!! ALL RIGHT !! THAT'S ONE TORTURE I CAN'T TAKE, YOU INHUMAN FIENDS !!! I'LL MARRY FAT FATIMA !!

THE DESERT ABODE OF THE WIDOW, FAT FATIMA.
WE BRING YOU GLAD TIDINGS OF INDESCRIBABLE ECSTASY, O SOON-TO-BE-ASTONISHED HAG ! YOUR FAITH IN MEN IS ABOUT TO BE RESTORED !
BAH ! I LOST MY FAITH IN ALL MANKIND WHEN THE BATHLESS ONE ESCAPED MY LOVING CLUTCHES 20 YEARS AGO !!

HE HAS COME BACK TO YOU, O FAT FATIMA—LOOK !
—'TIS YOU !!
KEERECT !! 'TIS ME, ALL RIGHT, BLARST YOU !!
Copr. 1943 by United Feature Syndicate, Inc.
Tm. Reg. U. S. Pat. Off.—All rights reserved
9-12
R. VAN BUREN

MY FAITH IN MEN IS RESTORED !! THERE IS SUCH A THING AS TRUE LOVE, AS YOUR RETURN PROVES !! I GIVE MY CONSENT TO THE MAHARAJAH'S MARRIAGE TO MY DAUGHTER !! WE WILL MAKE IT A DOUBLE WEDDING !

I'M SURE I DON'T KNOW WHAT SHE'S GOT THAT US 669 OTHER WIVES HAVEN'T GOT !!
QUIET !! THE WEDDING CEREMONY IS ABOUT TO BEGIN !
TO BE CONTINUED—

PSST— ONE WORD OF ADVICE — BEFORE THE NUPTIALS COMMENCE. THE MAHARAJAH'S OTHER 669 MARRIAGES ALL WENT ON THE ROCKS BECAUSE NOT ONE OF HIS WIVES UNDER— STOOD HIM. ALL HE WANTS OF A WIFE IS TO JUST LOOK AT HER. THE MINUTE A BRIDE APPROACHES HIM WITH A WIFELY KISS AS HER OBJECT, THE HONEYMOON IS OVER— AND SHE IS BANISHED TO THE HAREM FOREVER !!! THE MAHARAJAH IS STRICTLY A LOOKER — SEE ?
AHEM! WE WILL NOW BEGIN THE CEREMONY —

WAIT !!! I DISCOVERED THIS PACKAGE BROUGHT INTO HAMBURGISTAN BY THE BATHLESS ONE !!! IT IS AN INFERNAL MACHINE, NO DOUBT— PUT HIM TO DEATH !!!
HOLY SMOKES !!! THAT'S THE PROJECTION MACHINE WITH THE FILM IN IT I WAS DELIVERIN' WHEN I WAS SHANGHAIED IN CRAB- TREE CORNERS
9-19

THERE'S NOTHIN' DANGEROUS ABOUT THIS MACHINE, FOLKS— IT'S JUST A MOVIE PRO- JECTOR. I'LL SHOW YOU HOW IT WORKS

SEE !!!
THAT GORGEOUS ONE— WHO IS SHE?

WEDY LA STARR, O' COURSE!
CAN SHE LEAVE THE WALL?

NOPE !!! ALL YOU CAN DO IS JUST LOOK AT HER, BUB
SWAMI !!! I HAVE CHANGED MY MIND !!! I WILL NOT WED THIS CREATURE!! SHE'S JUST LIKE ALL THE REST. I HAVE DECIDED TO MARRY HER— WEDY LA STARR!

AT LAST I HAVE DISCOVERED THE PERFECT WIFE !!! NO NAGGING— NO ASK- ING FOR AFFECTION— NO JEALOUSY— AND ALWAYS AT MY BECK AND CALL! SHE IS MY IDEAL! COMMENCE THE CEREMONY !!!
YOU HAVE SPOKEN, O MAHARAJAH— AND I OBEY!

—AND SO I NOW PRONOUNCE YOU AND WEDY LA STARR, MAHARAJAH AND WIFE !!!
HOORAY !!! NOW I DON'T HAVE TO MARRY FAT FIFI—
'TIS DONE !

JUST MADE IT AGAIN !!! I AIN'T AS FAST AS I WAS 20 YEARS AGO — BUT (CHUCKLE !!!) NEITHER IS SHE !!!
R. VAN BUREN

ABBIE an' SLATS
RAEBURN VAN BUREN

LOVE COMES TO JASPER HAGSTONE---
IN ALL MY LIFE I HAVE NEVER MET ANY SO SWEET, SIMPLE, SO SHY AS SUSAN DEWDROP

I USED EVERY TERM OF ENDEARMENT KNOWN TO MAN! I PROMISED TO LOVE AND PROTECT HER UNTIL MY DYING DAY.
I PLEADED WITH HER TO BECOME MY WIFE!!! MY!! I DIDN'T KNOW I HAD SUCH ARDENT PHRASES IN ME
NEW YORK PAPERS JUST CAME IN, MR. HAGSTONE!

CHOKE!!
THE NEW WAR M

"SUING SUSIE" IS AT IT AGAI
"SUING SUSIE," WHO HAS CLEANED UP A FORTUNE SUING FOOLISH OLD MILLIONAIRES FOR BREACH OF PROMISE, TODAY FILED HER TWENTY-SEVENTH LAWSUIT, ON THE USUAL GROUNDS, AGAINST MA DRAKE P. GOUT, AGED TYCOON WHO NOT LONG AGO WAS SUED BY THE ATTRACTIVE SHOW-GIRL FRANCINE PIERRE LA FR
SUSAN DEWDROP

OH, THAT LETTER!! THAT LETTER!!

I DON'T CARE WHO YOU ARE!! ALL LETTERS ARE PROTECTED BY THE UNITED STATES MAIL--AND THEY GO TO THE PERSONS ADDRESSED!!
U.S.
Copr. 1942 by United Feature Syndicate, Inc.
Tm. Reg. U. S. Pat. Off.--All rights reserved

I MUST GET THAT LETTER!!!!
--HMM-- IT WOULD BE A SLIGHTLY ILLEGAL JOB--- SO. I MUST GET A SLIGHTLY ILLEGAL PERSON TO DO IT

SO YA SENT FOR ME!!!! WELL-- I'M READY FOR YA--YA OLD GASBAG!!! PUT 'EM UP!!!
MY DEAR BATHLESS!! I DON'T WANT TO DO YOU ANY HARM!! I--- WANT TO DO YOU SOME GOOD!! COME IN, OLD FRIEND---
R. VAN BUREN
3-8
TO BE CONTINUED....

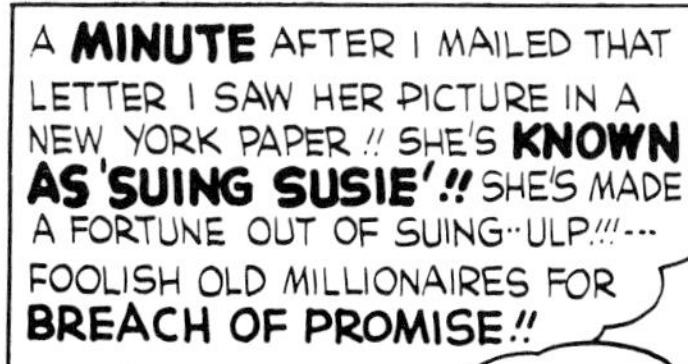

Copr. 1942 by United Feature Syndicate, Inc.
Tm. Reg. U. S. Pat. Off.—All rights reserved

CONTINUED FROM LAST WEEK---
I'M ALL READY TO TAKE YOU NIGHT-CLUBBING, J.P.!!
YOU ARE!!! GOLLY, THAT'S MIGHTY NICE O'YOU, MAM!!
3/22

THAT APE HAGSTONE TOLD ME SHE WAS A GOLD DIGGER!! AND YET HERE SHE IS, TREATING ME, A PAUPER, LIKE AS IF I WAS A MILLIONAIRE!! I'D GIVE THAT LETTER BACK TO HER IF HAGSTONE HADN'T PROMISED ME TEN BERRIES FOR IT

HOURS LATER---AFTER THE MOST WONDERFUL EVENING POP HAS EVER ENJOYED
AND HERE IS YOUR CHECK, SIR---EXACTLY NINETY DOLLARS
OH--- GIGGLE!! YOU'RE SO WITTY, J.P. GIVE IT TO HIM, WAITER---
GIVE IT TO HER--IT'S HER TREAT

B-BUT--- I HAVEN'T GOT THE CASH ON ME!!!
SILLY BOY!! ALL A MAN IN YOUR POSITION HAS TO DO IS SIGN THE CHECK!!

THIS IS SIGNED J.P. GROGGINS!!!
J.P. GROGGINS?? AREN'T YOU J.P. GROOPLE!! THE MILLION-AIRE!!
NO MAM, I'M J.P. GROGGINS, THE PAUPER.

INSOMANIA CLUB
PLUNK!

BACK HOME THE NEXT DAY---
YOU DID GET THE LETTER. THAT'S WON-DERFUL!! GIVE IT TO ME AND I'LL GIVE YOU THE TEN DOL-LARS!
HAGSTONE-- I HAPPENS TO KNOW YOU HAVE TWO OF THE ONLY BOTTLES OF BARLEYCORN'S PRIDE IN EXISTANCE. INSTEAD OF THE TEN-SPOT I'LL TAKE ONE OF THOSE PRECIOUS BOTTLES O'HEAV-ENLY NECTAR IN PAYMENT

SORRY TO HAVE KEPT YOU WAITING, OLD CHAP--BUT I HAD A HARD TIME FINDING THE BOTTLE AND THEN--- AHEM!! I HAD A LI'L BUSINESS TO ATTEND TO IN THE KITCHEN. I HOPE YOU DIDN'T MIND MY ABSENCE
NOT AT ALL, OLD CHAP. I USED IT TO A GOOD ADVANTAGE!!

HA-HA!! I TOOK THE PRE-CAUTION OF EMPTYING THE PRICELESS CONTENTS OF THAT QUART INTO A DECANTER, AND FILLED THAT BOTTLE WITH VINEGAR! THAT OAF WILL NEVER KNOW THE DIFFERENCE

WHILE THAT OAF WAS EMPTYING THAT BOTTLE INTO THE WINE DECANTER---I TOOK THE PRECAUTION OF SWIPING THE OTHER BOTTLE FROM THE CELLAR. HE'S TOO STINGY EVER TO DRINK IT, SO HE'LL NEVER KNOW THE DIFFERENCE!!
R. VAN BUREN

ABBIE an' SLATS by
RAEBURN VAN BUREN

POOL

YOU TOOK US BOYS FOR SEVEN POTATOES AND NINETY-FIVE CENTS. WHEW!!
I'VE GOTTA HAND IT TO YOU, BATHLESS. YOU CERTAINLY KNOW HOW TO ROLL THEM BONES
IT'S AN ART, BOYS-- SEE YOU TOMORROW!
IT'S AN ART, GENTLEMEN!!! SEE YOU TOMORROW!
YOU TOOK THAT TRUSTING EAST ROSEVILLE INDUSTRIAL CROWD FOR $70,000-- SPLENDID WORK, HAGSTONE!!
IT WAS A PLEASURE WATCHING YOU MANIPULATE THOSE STOCKS, OLD BOY!!
POOL HALL
BANK
POST NO BILLS

OUTA MY WAY, YE SLOPPY OLE GASBAG!!!
I WOULD LIKE TO GET BY. KINDLY STEP OFF INTO THE MUD. YOU SHOULD FEEL AT HOME THERE

ONE O'US IS GONNA GIT BY. THE OTHER AIN'T!!!
FORTUNATELY, I BROUGHT MY STOUTEST CANE!
BANK
5-23
Copr. 1943 by United Feature Syndicate, Inc.
Tm. Reg. U. S. Pat. Off.—All rights reserved

CONTROL YOURSELF, BATHLESS!!
I KNOW YOU!! IT'S WORTH IT-- BUT THINK O' BECKY!!
YOU'RE RIGHT-- IT'D BREAK HER HEART
YOU'LL GO BACK TO THE CLINK FOR ANOTHER TEN DAYS!

SOMEDAY--- SOMEHOW-- MEBBE I CAN WHALE THE LIVIN' DAYLIGHTS OUTA THAT BILIOUS, BANDY-LEGGED BLIMP--- LEGALLY!!!

OH--IF ONLY SOMEDAY I COULD OBEY MY NATURAL IMPULSE TO THRASH HIM WITHIN AN INCH OF HIS LIFE! BUT, UNFORTUNATELY, THERE ARE LAWS AGAINST THAT SORT OF THING!!
TWO MINDS WITH BUT A SINGLE YEARNING TO ASSAULT EACH OTHER--- WITHOUT BREAKING THE LAW. AND SO--FATE STEPS IN...          (TO BE CONTINUED)

SOME DAY—SOMEHOW— MEBBE I CAN WHALE THE LIVIN' DAYLIGHTS OUTA THAT BILIOUS BANDYLEGGED BLIMP— LEGALLY!

OH—IF ONLY SOME DAY I COULD OBEY MY NATURAL IMPULSE TO THRASH HIM WITHIN AN INCH OF HIS LIFE!! BUT, UNFORTUNATELY, THERE ARE LAWS AGAINST THAT SORT OF THING!
Copr. 1943 by United Feature Syndicate, Inc.
Tm. Reg. U. S. Pat. Off.—All rights reserved

THE SUMPTUOUS NEW YORK OFFICES OF THE RUTCH CLUTCH CORPORATION.
AND SO, GENTLEMEN—THE DEAL IS COMPLETED!!! IN BEHALF OF OUR STOCKHOLDERS I ACCEPT YOUR CHECK FOR $27,000,000 AND NOW RUTCH CLUTCH IS IN THE HANDS OF THE UNITED STATES GOVERNMENT!

DIVIDING THE MONEY WILL BE SIMPLE. THERE ARE ONLY TWO STOCKHOLDERS— THE PRESIDENT OF RUTCH CLUTCH, WHO OWNS THE MAJORITY OF STOCK—AND ONE AMOS P. CRATCHIT OF CRABTREE CORNERS, WHO OWNS (CHUCKLE) ONE TENTH OF ONE SHARE.

THE NEXT DAY.
I'VE CONTACTED CRABTREE CORNERS. AMOS P. CRATCHIT HAS BEEN DEAD 45 YEARS!!
HE LEFT A WILL, NATURALLY. TO WHOM DID HE BEQUEATH HIS ONE-TENTH OF ONE SHARE?

HE WAS AN ARDENT BOXING FAN. IN HIS PECULIAR WILL HE LEFT HIS TINY SHARE OF RUTCH CLUTCH TO THE TWELVE-YEAR-OLD SCHOOLBOY IN CRABTREE CORNERS MOST ADEPT AT FISTICUFFS!!

ACCORDING TO OLD RECORDS— TWO BOYS CAME UP TO FIGHT THE FINALS—LITTLE J. PIERPONT GROGGINS AND LITTLE JASPER HAGSTONE.
WELL, WHO WON?

THAT IS WHAT'S SO CONFUSING. NOBODY WON!!! JUST AS THE BOUT APPROACHED ITS CLIMAX— THE ELECTRIFYING NEWS CAME THAT THE UNITED STATES HAD DECLARED WAR ON SPAIN!!

ACCORDING TO THE NEWS-PAPERS—THE CROWD IN-STANTLY BROKE UP AND IN THE TUMULTUOUS EVENTS THAT FOLLOWED THE EPISODE WAS COMPLETELY FOR-GOTTEN!!
THAT ONE-TENTH OF A SHARE IS WORTH $10,000!!
5-30

IT IS TODAY— BUT RUTCH CLUTCH WAS IN ITS IN-FANCY THEN—ITS SHARES WERE OF A TRIVIAL VALUE
BUT GREAT SCOTT, MAN! WE CANNOT SETTLE THIS $27,000,000 DEAL UNTIL WE DETERMINE THE LEGAL OWNER OF THAT FRACTION OF A SHARE!!

THE TERMS OF OLD AMOS CRATCHIT'S WILL ARE UN-BREAKABLE!! THE ONLY WAY TO DETERMINE THE RIGHTFUL OWNER IS TO FINISH THAT 45 YEAR-OLD FIGHT!!
TO BE CONTINUED

YOU TWO ARE NOW GOOD FRIENDS, NO DOUBT, BUT I WONDER IF YOU BOTH RECALL THAT 45 YEARS AGO THE DEAREST WISH OF YOUR LITTLE HEARTS WAS TO WHALE THE DAYLIGHTS OUT OF EACH OTHER!
IT'S STILL THE DEAREST WISH O' M' HEART !!
MAN AND BOY—IT HAS ALWAYS BEEN MY FONDEST DREAM TO PULVERIZE THAT BARNACLED OLD SEA-RAT LEGALLY !!!

YOU STILL HATE EACH OTHER? SPLENDID !!! AND YOU STILL LONG TO COMMIT FELONIOUS ASSAULT UPON EACH OTHER—LEGALLY? NOTHING COULD BE MORE SUITABLE !!!
I DON'T GET IT!

45 YEARS AGO THE LATE AMOS P. CRATCHIT STIPULATED IN HIS WILL THAT ONE-TENTH OF ONE SHARE OF THE THEN INSIGNIFICANT RUTCH CLUTCH CORPORATION BE AWARDED TO THE YOUNGSTER MOST PROFICIENT IN FISTICUFFS
I RECALL IT NOW !! THAT RASCAL AND I WERE SELECTED TO FIGHT IT OUT.

KEERECT !!! AND JUST AS THE BOUT APPROACHED ITS CLIMAX COME THE NEWS THAT THE UNITED STATES HAD DECLARED WAR ON SPAIN !!! THE FIGHT WAS FORGOTTEN IN TH' EXCITEMENT !!
EXACTLY! THE ISSUE WAS NEVER DECIDED !!! AND TODAY THAT ONE-TENTH OF ONE SHARE IS WORTH $10,000 !!!

AND THERE IS NO LEGAL WAY TO GIVE THAT MONEY TO ANYONE—EXCEPT TO THE WINNER OF THAT 46-YEAR-OLD UNFINISHED FIGHT !!
I'M WILLIN' T' FINISH IT—RIGHT NOW!
SO AM I !! NOT ONLY FOR THE TEN THOUSAND—BUT FOR THE SHEER JOY OF BEATING THAT UNWASHED SCOUNDREL'S BRAINS OUT !!!

GENTLEMEN !! FIGHTING IT OUT HERE WOULD BE A COMMON BRAWL AND RESULT IN COURT ACTION. THIS CONTEST MUST BE CONDUCTED ACCORDING TO THE CRATCHIT WILL, ON A SPORTING BASIS IN AN OFFICIAL RING!

TREE CORNERS COURI
GIGANTIC NEWSPAPER SERVICE
JUNE 5, 1943
BANKER HAGSTONE TO SLUG IT OUT WITH BATHLESS GROGGINS
FIGHT TO A FINISH WILL OCCUR NEXT SUNDAY AT CRABTREE CORNERS ARENA !! OLD-TIMERS SAY THIS WILL BE THE LONGEST DELAYED GRUDGE FIGHT IN FISTICUFFS ANNALS---
TO BE CONTINUED.

CRABTREE CORNERS
BATHLESS GROGGINS OUTLINES SPECTACULAR PLAN IF HE WINS $10,000 BOUT.
"WHEN THE $10,000 IS AWARDED TO ME AFTER MY SLAUGHTER OF JASPER HAGSTONE NEXT SUNDAY, I PLAN TO GO INTO BUSINESS WITH MY VERY CLOSE FRIEND, HAGGIS MCBAGPIPE, EMINENT PIG...

Copr. 1943 by United Feature Syndicate, Inc.
Tm. Reg. U. S. Pat. Off. — All rights reserved

THE NIGHT BEFORE THE FIGHT...
JASPER, OLD CHUM-THERE IS A SECRET CONCERNING MY FOUL COUSIN, BATHLESS GROGGINS, THAT NO ONE KNOWS BUT ME-A SECRET THAT'LL WIN THIS FIGHT FOR YOU!!
YES ?

40 YEARS AGO BATHLESS GROGGINS WAS SHIPWRECKED ON THE MOST LOATHESOME SPOT ON EARTH-GOAT ISLAND-A PLACE INHABITED EXCLUSIVELY BY THE LOWEST TYPE OF GOAT-THOUSANDS OF 'EM !!

WHEN HE WAS, UNFORTUNATELY, RESCUED HE HAD ACQUIRED THAT DREAD MALADY-THE SEVENTEEN-YEAR ITCH !! THERE IS NO CURE EXCEPT ONE : THE VICTIM MUST COME IN CONTACT WITH A SECOND PARTY WHO IS SUSCEPTIBLE

IN THAT CASE-THE SECOND PARTY ABSORBS THE 17-YEAR ITCH FROM THE FIRST PARTY, LEAVING THE ORIGINAL VICTIM ITCHLESS !! BUT HA-HA !!! ONLY ONE IN TEN MILLION IS SUSCEPTIBLE AND SO MY POOR COUSIN SUFFERED THE FULL 17 YEARS !!

AND-IF EVER BATHLESS COMES INTO CONTACT AGAIN WITH ANYTHING PERTAINING TO GOATS-THE 17-YEAR ITCH WILL COME BACK !!
AHA !! I BEGIN TO SEE YOUR POINT !

A BIT OF, SAY, POWDERED GOAT'S MILK ON YOUR GLOVE-A QUICK JAB TO HIS NOSE-HE SNIFFS IT-AND-WHAM !!-BATHLESS BECOMES A WRITHING, SCRATCHING, HELPLESS MASS !!
HA-HA !!!-AND REMAINS THAT WAY-FOR HO-HO-17 YEARS !! SPLENDID, WILBERFORCE, SPLENDID !!

THE NIGHT OF THE FIGHT
DON'T SCRATCH, GROGGINS !! FIGHT !

SOCK!
Copr. 1943 by United Feature Syndicate, Inc.
Tm. Reg. U. S. Pat. Off.—All rights reserved

THE WINNAH !! OF THE FIGHT AND OF THE GRAND PRIZE OF ONE TENTH OF ONE SHARE OF THE RUTCH CLUTCH CO.!!
SO IT'S SETTLED NOW THAT YOU'RE THE OWNER OF THE SHARE !! THAT'S FINE!! YOU'RE UNDER ARREST !

THE RUTCH CLUTCH WAS FRAUDULENTLY SOLD TO THE U.S. GOVERNMENT FOR $25,000,000. AS OWNER OF ONE TENTH OF ONE SHARE-YOU, SIR, ARE LIABLE TO A FINE OF $10,000-OR TEN YEARS IN JAIL !!
(CHOKE !!!) I'LL PAY THE FINE. BUT, BLAST IT ! -I'M ITCHIN' ALL OVER
6-27

AND ME- I'M NOT ITCHIN' ANYMORE !!
I'M ONE IN (SOB) TEN MILLION !

ABBIE an' SLATS by
RAEBURN VAN BUREN

THAT'S THE DEAL, GROGGINS! WE AGREE NOT TO RE-OPEN THE BUMBOAT BARNEY CASE — IF YOU AGREE TO PERSUADE THE MAHARAJA OF SCRATCHISTAN, HASSAN THE UNWASHED, TO PERMIT DUCKY-WUCKY TO ADVERTISE IN SCRATCH-ISTAN!
YE AIN'T ASKIN' ME T' PERSUADE 'EM T' USE TH' STUFF, ARE YE?

A WEEK OR SO LATER — THE HARBOR OF ITCHOPOLIS, CAPITAL OF SCRATCHISTAN.
BEHOLD! A FIRE-BREATHING VESSEL FROM OUT OF THIS WORLD APPROACHES!
BEHOLD THE LAUGHABLE FACES OF THE FOREIGN DEVILS! SUCH UNHEALTHY COLOR CAUSED BY THEIR ADDICTION TO SOAP!
THEY THINK THEY ARE SIGHTSEEING! LO — ONE OF THE FOREIGN DEVILS COMETH!
??? DOES HE NOT KNOW IT IS FORBIDDEN TO ANY OUTSIDER TO ENTER SCRATCH-ISTAN?

BOYS! I'M NO OUTSIDER! I'M ONE O' YOU! DON'T ANY O' YE RECOGNIZE ME?
?? YES! 'TIS HE!! MINE EYES HAVE NOT FEASTED UPON HIM FOR TWO SCORE YEARS!

'TIS THE BATHLESS ONE! A BROTHER UNDER THE SKIN! ONE WHO BELIEVES AS WE DO! WELCOME!
IS HASSAN THE UNWASHED STILL TH' MAHARAJA?

AYE — STILL THE MAHARAJA — AND STILL UNWASHED! HIS STRENGTH GROWETH WITH THE YEARS.
Copr. 1947 by United Feature Syndicate, Inc.
Tm. Reg. U. S. Pat. Off.—All rights reserved
1-19

WELCOME BACK! I KNEW YOU WERE COMING BY THE WIND!!
TO BE CONTINUED

WHEN GREEK MEETS GREEK, OR THE REUNION OF THOSE BROTHERS UNDER THE SKIN—BATHLESS GROGGINS AND HASSAN THE UNWASHED...
'TIS GOOD TO FEAST MINE EYES UPON YOU, O BATHLESS ONE! ALTHOUGH YOU HAVE SPENT LO, THESE MANY YEARS AMONGST THE UNBELIEVING—A SINGLE GLANCE TELLS ME YOU HAVE BEEN FAITHFUL TO OUR IDEALS! BATHLESS YOU DEPARTED AND BATHLESS YOU RETURN! HAVE A CIGAR! HAVE A DOZEN DANCING GIRLS!
THANKS, PAL—BUT WHEN YE FIND OUT WHY I'VE COME—YE MIGHT FEEL DIFF'RENTLY ABOUT ME.

THE ONLY WAY WE SCRATCHISTANIANS COULD FEEL DIFFERENTLY ABOUT YOU IS TO LOVE YOU MORE. YOUR LOYALTY HAS BEEN UNSWERVING--

--TO OUR EARTHLY PHILOSOPHY, OR NATURAL WAY OF LIFE! YOU, WHO HAVE LIVED LONG AMONG SOAP FANATICS, HAVE RETURNED TO US AS IMPURE AS THE DAY YOU LEFT!
Copr. 1947 by United Feature Syndicate, Inc.
Tm. Reg. U. S. Pat. Off.—All rights reserved

HAVE ANOTHER CIGAR! HAVE ANOTHER 20 DANCING GIRLS!
HOLD IT, PAL! I CAN'T TAKE ALL THESE PRESENTS UNTIL I MAKES A CLEAN BREAST OF IT, IF YOU'LL EXCUSE TH' EXPRESSION.

DO YOU REMEMBER—"BUMBOAT BARNEY"?
AYE! MANY TIMES HAVE I CHUCKLED OVER THE DELIGHTFUL WAY IN WHICH THAT INDIVIDUAL WAS HANDLED.

WELL, A COUPLE O' FELLAS BACK HOME FOUND OUT ABOUT THAT. AFTER ALL THESE YEARS! IF THEY HAS THE CASE RE-OPENED--I'M A DEAD DUCK!
YOU MEAN—WHERE YOU COME FROM, SUCH A WORTHY DEED IS REGARDED AS A CRIME?
1-26

KEERECT! AND THEY'LL GET ME, PAL, ONLESS YOU MAKES THE SUPREME SACRIFICE FOR ME!
JUST NAME IT, O GROGGINS, AND 'TIS DONE!
THERE IS NOTHING BENEATH THE SUN YOU COULD ASK OF US THAT WOULD BE TOO MUCH.
DO YOU WANT OUR FORTUNES, OUR LOVED ONES, OUR LIVES?

I WANTS MORE THAN THAT, CHUMS-- I WANTS YOU TO ALLOW SOAP INTO SCRATCHISTAN!
R. VAN BUREN—
--A STUNNED SILENCE! EYES THAT GLOWED WITH WARM AFFECTION FREEZE INTO UNBELIEVABLE HORROR---
TO BE CONTINUED...

OLD FRIEND—TO SAVE YOUR LIFE, YOU ASK ME TO ALLOW THE FORBIDDEN FRUIT, SOAP, INTO SCRATCHISTAN?
FORGET IT! I LOST MY HEAD. SAY NO, OLE PAL—AND I'LL UNDERSTAND. I'LL GO BACK TO AMERICA AN' FACE TH' MUSIC!

OLD FRIEND, I WILL NOT GIVE YOU A DEFINITE ANSWER MYSELF! THE IMPERIAL COUNCIL MEETS IN A MONTH. GO HOME—AND AWAIT OUR DECISION.

NEW YORK— THE REPRESENTATIVES OF THE DUCKY WUCKY SOAP CO.
WELL, GROGGINS, DID YOU SUCCEED?
WILL DUCKY WUCKY SOAP PENETRATE THE IRON CURTAIN OF SCRATCHISTAN?
G

OR DID YOU FAIL?
AND WILL WE BE FORCED TO CALL THE ATTENTION OF THE AUTHORITIES TO A CERTAIN EPISODE IN YOUR PAST?
I FAILED!

IT AIN'T OFFICIAL YET. WE'LL KNOW THE ANSWER IN A MONTH—BUT I CAN TELL YOU WHAT IT'LL BE IN JUST TWO WORDS—"NO SOAP"!
WE'LL GIVE YOU A BREAK, GROGGINS! WE'LL WAIT OUT THE MONTH—FOR THE OFFICIAL ANSWER.

EASTERN UNION TELEGRAM
TO
J. PIERPONT GROGGINS
CRABTREE CORNERS—
SCRATCHISTAN'S ANSWER SAVES YOU! RECEIVED OFFICIAL PERMISSION TO PUT UP TEN THOUSAND ADVERTISING SIGNS... CONGRATULATIONS.
THE DUCKY WUCKY SOAP CO.

IT JUST DON'T ADD UP! SCRATCHISTAN IS ANTI-SOAP. ALLUS HAS BEEN. NOTHIN' NO SCRATCHISTANIANS HATE OR FEARS MORE'N SOAP! WHAT COULD THEY POSSIBLY WANT SOAP ADS FOR?
2-2
R. VAN BUREN

THERE'S NOTHING LIKE— DUCKY WUCKY SOAP!
OBEY OUR LAWS OR THIS WILL HAPPEN TO YOU!
FLASH— SCRATCHISTAN!
AH, 'TIS A WISE DECREE OF HASSAN THE UNWASHED THAT ALL OTHER PUNISHMENT FOR CRIME BE ABOLISHED!
AND ONLY ONE PUNISHMENT REMAINS FOR ANY CRIME—THE ONE PICTURED IN THAT HIDEOUS, FRIGHTENING, BLOOD-CURDLING SIGN!
SINCE THOSE SIGNS WENT UP, ALL CRIME IN SCRATCHISTAN HAS VANISHED!
Copr. 1947 by United Feature Syndicate, Inc.
Tm. Reg. U. S. Pat. Off.—All rights reserved

ABBIE an' SLATS by
RAEBURN VAN BUREN

THE EXPERIMENTAL LABORATORIES OF A GREAT PERFUME COMPANY NEAR CRABTREE CORNERS····
AT LAST! MY FORTY YEARS OF RESEARCH HAVE ENDED IN THE DISCOVERY OF THE VERY ULTIMATE IN AROMATIC FASCINATION

A PERFUME SO POWERFUL — SO DEVASTATING — THAT LAWS MAY BE PASSED AGAINST IT! I DARE NOT RELEASE IT TO THE INNOCENT PUBLIC UNTIL I KNOW ITS FULL EFFECTIVENESS!

I'D BE A MARTYR TO SCIENCE AND TRY IT ON MYSELF — BUT I'M A WEAK OLD MAN. HOW COULD I FIGHT OFF THE THUNDERING HERDS OF LOVE-FRENZIED GIRLS? I'LL SUBMIT IT TO THE BOARD OF DIRECTORS — WITH A WARNING!

THE BOARD OF DIRECTORS MEETS····
GENTLEMEN! THIS IS A SOLEMN MOMENT IN THE HISTORY OF SMELL. OUR LABORATORIES HAVE EVOLVED A PERFUME SO IRRESISTIBLE--

--THAT ITS WEARER STANDS IN GREAT DANGER OF BEING TRAMPLED TO DEATH.! WE MUST BE CAREFUL TO TRY IT ON AN EMPLOYEE WHOSE LIFE IS OF NO GREAT VALUE TO OUR STOCKHOLDERS·

WHAT ARE YOU DOING HERE?
I'VE GOTTA CLEAN OUT TH' JOINT. THAT'S MY JOB, BUB. YOU GO AHEAD AN' DO YOURS!

A MOPMAN! CAN ANYTHING BE OF LESS VALUE TO THE STOCKHOLDERS?
CAN ANYONE BE MORE EASILY REPLACED?
THE MEETING IS ADJOURNED! LET'S GO!

HEY!
Copr. 1949 by United Feature Syndicate, Inc.
Tm. Reg. U. S. Pat. Off.—All rights reserved
TO BE CONTINUED

TO BE CONTINUED

WHAT MORE PROOF DOES THEM BLARSTED CHEMISTS NEED TO TEST THEIR PERFUME -- IMAGINE THEM CHASIN' OL' BATHLESS AN' FINDIN' ME IRRESISTIBLE.

ALL MEN ARE RATS, MABEL -- I'LL NEVER LOOK AT ANOTHER OF THEM WORMS SO LONG AS I LIVE -- (SNIFF!) (SNIFF!)
LIKEWISE, DEARIE, THERE AIN'T NO TORTURE HORRIBLE ENOUGH TO BRING ME EVEN CLOSE TO A -- (SNIFF!) (SNIFF!)

OUT OF A JOB AGAIN AND DEAD BROKE. OLD AND FRIENDLESS. NO ONE T'SAY A KIND OR LOVIN' WORD T'A BROKEN-DOWN OLD FAILURE -- (CHOKE!)

LOVER!
DREAMBOAT!
POLICE!

LAST-MILE MILTON, THE DEATH HOUSE LOUSE
VS
BLACK DEATH BENNY, THE WRESTLER'S DOOM
IN THE GRUDGE MATCH OF THE CENTURY
CRABTREE CORNERS STADIUM

CUSTOMERS ARE REQUESTED TO REMAIN FOR THE FINAL SERVICES AS GUESTS O' THE MANAGEMENT, SHOULD ONE OF THE CONTESTANTS FAIL TO SURVIVE. I THANK YOUSE.
BRRRRRR! IT'S NOTHIN' BUT LEGAL MOIDER, UNLEASHIN' THEM TWO BEASTS IN TH' SAME RING!
ZZZZZZZZ

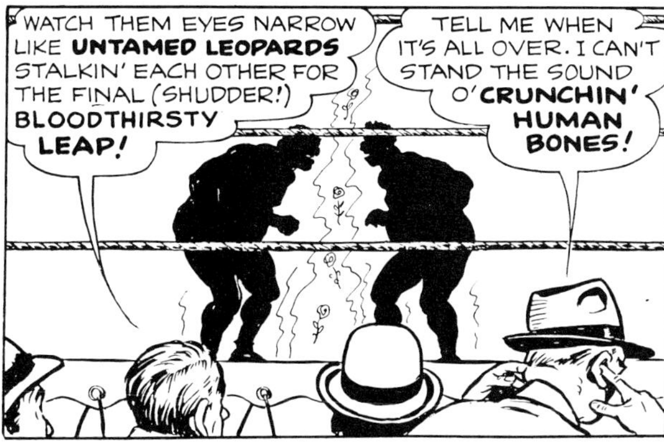
WATCH THEM EYES NARROW LIKE UNTAMED LEOPARDS STALKIN' EACH OTHER FOR THE FINAL (SHUDDER!) BLOODTHIRSTY LEAP!
TELL ME WHEN IT'S ALL OVER. I CAN'T STAND THE SOUND O'CRUNCHIN' HUMAN BONES!

CAN YOUSE (SNIFF!) EVER FORGIVE ME FOR FRACTURIN' YER SKULL IN PHILADELPHIA, BLACK DEATH?
A THOUSAND TIMES YES, (SNIFF!) LAST-MILE MILTON -- IF YOUSE'LL ONLY WHISPER T'ME THAT YOUSE AIN'T HELD A GRUDGE FOR THE TIME I CRUSHED YOUR COLLARBONE IN OMAHA!
4-17

(YAWNN!) HOW DO THEM HYENAS EXPECT A FELLER T' REST MAKIN' ALL THAT BLARSTED RACKET?
EXIT
TO BE CONTINUED

Copr. 1949 by United Feature Syndicate, Inc.
Tm. Reg. U.S. Pat. Off.—All rights reserved

OBSERVE, GENTLEMEN--TWO HOURS AGO I SQUIRTED A SINGLE DROP OF "AH-H-H-H," OUR NEW PERFUME, ON THIS EXPERIMENTAL RAT. THE OTHER RATS IMMEDIATELY FELL MADLY IN LOVE WITH HER--SHOWERED HER WITH GIFTS OF RANCID CHEESE AND DECAYED WALNUT SHELLS. SHE WAS THE QUEEN OF THE LAB--B-BUT (CHOKE.!!) THEN IT H-HAPPENED.!!
FOR HEAVEN'S SAKE, WHAT HAPPENED?

SEE FOR YOURSELVES-- NOTHING LEFT BUT (UGH.!) A PITIFUL PILE OF BONES.! THEY SUDDENLY TURNED ON HER IN A FRENZY-- IT WAS HORRIBLE!!

THAT CAN ONLY MEAN THAT IN TWENTY MINUTES THE UNSANITARY OLD APE WE SQUIRTED WITH "AH-H-H-H"-- (SHUDDER.!!) WILL BE TORN LIMB FROM LIMB.!!
AND TO THINK IT MIGHT HAVE BEEN SOMEONE HUMAN LIKE ONE OF US.!!

MEANWHILE, POP IS STILL IGNORANT OF THE DOOM WHICH HANGS OVER HIS SWEET-SMELLING HEAD--
I'VE BEEN HERE FOR SEVEN WEEKS WAITING TO FLING MYSELF AND A DIAMOND NECKLACE AT HER GORGEOUS FEET.!!
GLADYS ALLURE
THE MOST DESIRABLE WOMAN IN THE WORLD IN MOROCCO MADNESS
STAGE ENTRANCE
BEGINNER!! I'VE FOLLOWED HER AROUND THE WORLD SIX TIMES--OFFERED HER ANYTHING MY FATHER'S MONEY CAN BUY--BUT (GROAN.!) SHE LAUGHED AT ME.!!
Copr. 1949 by United Feature Syndicate, Inc.
Tm. Reg. U. S. Pat. Off.—All rights reserved

BEAT IT, BOYS.! MISS ALLURE DON'T WANT NONE O' YOUSE GUYS TOSSIN' CHUNKS O' DIAMONDS IN HER DELICATELY BEAUTIFUL FACE--
STAGE EN
IF I DIE AS A RESULT OF THIS BRUTAL ATTACK, I'VE WILLED EVERYTHING I OWN TO YOU, GLADYS, MY LOVE.!!

HAVE THE SIDEWALKS CLEARED BEFORE I RETURN, BOYS--AND DUMP ALL THOSE CHEAP JEWELS IN THE GARBAGE CAN--

WHY DO I LOATHE ALL MEN SO (SNIFF.!! SNIFF.!!)--WHY DO I SUDDENLY FEEL WEAK IN THE KNEES--IT'S YOU--YOU BEAUTIFUL SPECIMEN--YOU GORGEOUS HUNK OF MANHOOD. GLADYS ALLURE IS IN LOVE AT LAST.!!
THERE'S NO USE FLATTERIN' ME, MAM--IT STANDS T' REASON--

I'M YOURS, UN- BELIEVABLE YOU, THE ONLY MAN TO MAKE MY HEART BEAT FASTER-- DON'T LET HIM ESCAPE, BOYS.!!
WE WON'T-- WE CAN'T UNDER- STAND WHY, BUT WE WON'T.!!
SMACK
5-1

IN TEN MINUTES THAT OLD MAN WILL BE BEATEN TO A BLOODY PULP BY HIS FORMER ADMIRERS.!!
TO BE CONTINUED ~

THE PERFUME FACTORY NEAR CRABTREE CORNERS...
IN PRECISELY TEN MINUTES THE OLD GOAT WE SQUIRTED WITH "AH-H-H-H," OUR FABULOUS NEW PERFUME, WILL LOSE HIS IRRESISTIBLE CHARM AND BE TORN LIMB FROM LIMB BY HIS FORMER ADMIRERS!!
AND TO THINK (SHUDDER!!) THIS MIGHT HAVE HAPPENED TO SOMEONE HUMAN!!

BUT, GLADYS, MY LOVE-SQUANDERING YOUR EXQUISITE BEAUTY ON THAT REPULSIVE OLD MOOSEFACE!!
THERE ARE OTHER THINGS IN A GIRL'S LIFE BESIDES DIAMONDS, JIM!!

OTHER THINGS ??-WHAT ARE YOU HINTING AT, GLADYS?
THE SOFT PURR OF HIS BREATH AS IT COMES SIFTING THROUGH HIS MUSTACHE...

THE REFLECTION OF MY FACE IN HIS PASSIONATELY PINK NOSE - THE SOUND OF HIS MUSCULAR KNEES BEATING A RYTHMIC LOVE CHANT ONE AGAINST THE OTHER... (SIGH!!)

NEVER, IN TWENTY YEARS OF TAILORING, HAVE I SEEN A FIGURE TO MATCH YOURS.!! MISS ALLURE IS SURE A LUCKY WOMAN!!

THOSE SHOULDERS-THAT WAIST-SUCH CARRIAGE-WHAT AN (UGH.!!) AIR.!!
NONE O' YER INSINU-ATIONS, BUB!!

Copr. 1949 by United Feature Syndicate, Inc.
Tm. Reg. U. S. Pat. Off.—All rights reserved
HIS TIME -IS (QUIVER!!) UP!!
R-RING!!

IT'S WHEN I'M NEAR YOU, LOVER BOY, THAT YOUR BEAUTY ROBS ME OF MY SENSES-I CAN'T SEE-OR HEAR-OR-(SNIFF.!! SNIFF.!!)

BUT THERE'S NOTHING WRONG WITH MY SENSE OF SMELL, YOU REPULSIVE OLD RAT-GET OUT OF HERE!!

I'LL MURDER THE OLD BUM - HE HYPNOTIZED ME.!!
HAVIN' THE DOUBTFUL CHOICE O' BEIN' MARRIED T' A MOODY WOMAN LIKE GLADYS OR BEIN' ALIVE, I NATURALLY PRE-FERS THE LATTER. S'LONG, GLADYS, HONEY!!
5-8
R. Van Buren

ABBIE an' SLATS by RAEBURN VAN BUREN

THE OFFICE OF BUD TEAGLE, POOL PARLOR TYCOON OF CRABTREE CORNERS
I'VE GOTTA RUSH OUT FOR AN HOUR, BATHLESS. BE A GOOD FELLER AND ANSWER THE PHONE FOR ME!!!
KEERECT!
GINGER ALE

GLUB!!! I'M THIRSTY!! HA!! GINGER ALE!!!

AN HOUR OR SO LATER
Stayed until five—Had to leave. No calls. Your Pal Groggins
RING

HELLO, TEAGLE—THIS IS PROFESSOR GRAVES. MIGHTY NICE OF YOU TO ALLOW ME TO KEEP THAT BOTTLE OF H2347 IN YOUR OFFICE WHILE I WAS IN TOWN. I AM LEAVING NOW—AND WILL DROP BY AND PICK IT UP!!!

I'VE BEEN NERVOUS AS A CAT, KNOWING THAT IN THAT INNOCENT-LOOKING GINGER ALE BOTTLE IS A LIQUID SO DEADLY THAT ANYTHING IT TOUCHES WILL COMPLETELY DISINTEGRATE WITHIN 30 DAYS!!!
NO TROUBLE AT ALL, PROFESSOR. I'LL BE WAITING FOR YOU!!!
1-28-45

TEAGLE, OLD MAN!!! YOU LOOK SICK!!!
P-PROFESSOR!!! I J-JUST MURDERED A PAL O'MINE—AN INNOCENT, T-TRUSTIN' P-PAL!!!

WHERE'S THE CORPSE?
IT AIN'T A CORPSE YET! BUT IT W-WILL BE!! IN 30 DAYS—JUST LIKE YOU SAID!! LOOK! THE BOTTLE!! IT'S EMPTY!!!
GINGER ALE
Copr. 1945 by United Feature Syndicate, Inc.
Tm. Reg. U. S. Pat. Off.—All rights reserved

EGAD!!! SO IT IS!!! WHERE IS THE DEATH-DEALING LIQUID?
INSIDE MY (SOB) PAL—BATHLESS GROGGINS! AND IT'S MY FAULT!! I ASKED HIM TO LOOK AFTER MY OFFICE WHILE I WAS GONE! I DIDN'T WARN HIM THAT DEATH LURKED WITHIN THIS BOTTLE!!! NATURALLY—IT BEING A WARM AFTERNOON—HE DRANK IT!!!

THEN HE WILL DISINTEGRATE COMPLETELY—IN 30 DAYS!!! NO POWER ON EARTH CAN SAVE HIM!!!
I AS GOOD AS MURDERED HIM!! BUT AT LEAST I CAN MAKE HIS LAST DAYS ON EARTH (SOB) HAPPY ONES!!

BUD TEAGLE CALLS EVERY MERCHANT IN TOWN INTO A CONFERENCE
AND SO—BATHLESS GROGGINS HAS JUST 30 DAYS TO LIVE!!! AND IT'S (SOB) MY FAULT!! I WANT HIS LAST DAYS TO BE H-HAPPY! ANYTHING HE WANTS, BOYS—GIVE HIM!! AND SEND THE BILLS TO ME!! I'LL MAKE CRABTREE CORNERS A LITTLE HEAVEN ON EARTH FOR HIM IF IT BANKRUPTS ME!!! BUT REMEMBER, BOYS—HE MUST NEVER KNOW WHY!!! IT WOULD SPOIL HIS PLEASURE!!
TO BE CONTINUED —

CONTINUED FROM LAST WEEK
AND SO, BATHLESS GROGGINS HAS JUST 30 DAYS TO LIVE! AND IT'S (SOB) MY FAULT! I WANT HIS LAST DAYS TO BE H-HAPPY! ANYTHING HE WANTS, BOYS, GIVE HIM! AND SEND THE BILLS TO ME!! I'LL MAKE CRABTREE CORNERS A LITTLE HEAVEN ON EARTH FOR HIM EVEN IF IT BANK-RUPTS ME! BUT REMEMBER, BOYS, HE MUST NEVER KNOW WHY!!! IT WOULD SPOIL HIS PLEASURE!!!

THE NEXT MORNING, POP AWAKES TO FACE HIS USUAL HAPHAZARD, CATCH-AS-CATCH-CAN EXISTENCE.
NO COFFEE!! (SIGH) I'LL HAFTA CHISEL BREAKFAST AGAIN!! HMM—WHAT RAZZLE-DAZZLE HAVEN'T I PULLED ON BICARB BENNY LATELY?
COFFEE

AT BICARB BENNY'S
I FEELS IN A SPORTIN' MOOD THIS MORNIN', BENNY! I'LL FLIP FOR COFFEE AN' DOUGHNUTS! HEADS IT'S FOR FREE—TAILS I PAYS!!!
THAT PENNY GOT HEADS ON BOTH SIDES, AIN'T IT, BATHLESS?
2-4-45

—CHOKE!!! KEERECT!!! WELL—LET'S PROCEED TOWARD THE COFFEE AN' DOUGHNUTS BY A DIFF'RENT CHANNEL. NOW, FIGGERIN' A CUP O' COFFEE IS WORTH SAY 20 DISHES AND A---
NO USE GOIN' ON WITH YOUR FIGGERIN', BATHLESS! THERE'LL BE NO COFFEE AN' DOUGHNUTS FOR YOU, THIS MORNING!

HEY, JAKE! A DOUBLE SIRLOIN STEAK, FRENCH FRIES, APPLE PIE A LA MODE AN' JAVA!!
NO, BENNY! THAT'LL COME TO A MILLION DISHES! I REFUSES TO SPEND THE REST O' MY LIFE IN THE KITCHEN!!

THERE'LL BE NO CHARGE, BATHLESS!! YOU'RE MY GUEST AND STICK THIS FINE HAVANA CIGAR IN YOUR POCKET! I'M DOING ALL THIS 'CAUSE I LIKES YOU, OLD PAL!!
(POOR BENNY HAS GONE OUT O' HIS MIND!! I'LL EAT QUICK AN SHOVE OFF BEFORE HE GETS REAL VIOLENT!)

THE LAST THING BENNY SAID TO ME WAS, "BE SURE AND COME BACK AND BE MY GUEST TONIGHT—ROAST BEEF WITH ALL THE FIXIN'S"! HE'LL BE IN A PADDED CELL BEFORE MORNIN'!!!
ROOM
BENNY'S LUNCH
Copr. 1945 by United Feature Syndicate, Inc.
Tm. Reg. U. S. Pat. Off.—All rights reserved

PASSION'S PAWN!!! SOUNDS VERY ENTERTAININ'! HMM—THE COAST IS CLEAR—
PASSION'S PAWN
NOW PLAYING

(CHOKE!) YOU GOT ME! NOW, BE A PAL AN' KICK ME ON TH' LEFT SIDE! THE ONE YOU GAVE ME ON THE RIGHT SIDE LAST NIGHT—STILL HURTS!!
KICK YOU?—DON'T BE REDICK, OLD PAL!!
CAMEO THEATER
PASSION'S PAWN
NOW PLAYING

I HOPE YOU ENJOY THIS SEAT, BATHLESS! — — AND IF ANYONE OBJECTS TO YOUR CRUNCHING THESE PEANUTS AND POPCORN— WE'LL EJECT HIM, AND BE SURE AND STOP IN AT THE BOX-OFFICE ON YOUR WAY OUT! THERE'S A 30-DAY PASS WAITING FOR YOU THERE!!
ANOTHER OLD CHUM GONE STARK, RAVING MAD!!! MUST BE AN EPIDEMIC!!
TO BE CONTINUED—

• CONTINUED FROM LAST WEEK •
GROGGINS HAD STEAK AND PIE A LA MODE FOR BREAKFAST, ROAST BEEF FOR LUNCH AND TURKEY FOR DINNER. HIS FIRST DAY'S EATIN' COMES TO $9.85
I INSISTED THAT HE ATTEND THE MATINEE; ALSO, I PRESENTED HIM WITH A MONTH'S PASS. HERE'S MY BILL — $15.00
AT THE RATE HE'S GOIN' HE'LL BANKRUPT ME!!!

BUT (SOB) GROGGINS WOULDN'T BE A WALKING CORPSE IF IT WERE'NT FOR ME!!! I LEFT HIM ALONE HERE, NOT WARNING HIM THAT IN THAT INNOCENT-LOOKING GINGER-ALE BOTTLE WAS — H 2347!!!

A LIQUID SO DANGEROUS THAT IN 30 DAYS GROGGINS WILL DISINTEGRATE COMPLETELY!!! NOTHING CAN SAVE HIM!!! THE LEAST I CAN DO IS MAKE HIS LAST MONTH ON EARTH HIS HAPPIEST. BUT HE DOES'NT KNOW WHY, SUDDENLY, HE CAN HAVE EVERYTHING IN TOWN! I'D SPOIL HIS PLEASURE!

EVERYBODY IN THIS TOWN HAS GONE SUDDENLY STARK RAVIN' MAD. THE PROOF OF THAT IS — EVERYONE IN TOWN IS SUDDENLY ACTIN' DECENT TO ME!!

MY! THAT'S A SLICK SUIT!
TOM!! DICK!! HARRY!! IT'S GROGGINS!! WE GOT HIM!!!
COLLEGE CUT CLOTHES SHOPPE
OUR ANNUAL SALE NOW GOING ON !!!

LEMME ALONE, BLARST YOU!!! I KNOW YOU WARNED ME NOT T'HANG AROUND IN FRONT O' YOUR WINDOW ON ACCOUNT IT DRIVES TRADE AWAY — BUT —

— I WAS JUST WALKIN' BY, I TELL YA!!
2-11-45

THERE NOW! A FINER FIT A KING COULDN'T HAVE!!!
I DON'T KNOW WHAT THIS IS ALL ABOUT — BUT I LOVE IT!

DON'T BE ASTONISHED, PRUNELLA, MY PET, IF I AM CIVIL TO GROGGINS. HE DOESN'T REALIZE IT — BUT EVERYONE KNOWS — PSST-PSST-PSST!!
OH, NO, JASPER! JUST 30 DAYS AND THEN, POUFF !!!?

I PREFER TO WALK THE REST OF THE WAY HOME WITH MR. GROGGINS, JASPER!! AND DON'T BOTHER CALLING ON ME TONIGHT. WE'LL BE BUSY, WON'T WE, MR. GROGGINS, DEAR !!!
BUT — YOU'RE MY FIANCEE!! — ER — BRFSK-AH-YES --- OF COURSE!! I UNDERSTAND!!!
TO BE CONTINUED

HOWDY, JASPER!!! HOW COME YOU'RE HANGIN' AROUND OUTSIDE YOUR FIANCÉE'S HOME?
BECAUSE MY FIANCÉE IS IN THERE—(CHOKE!!) SPOONIN' WITH ANOTHER MAN!!!

WELL, WHY DON'T YOU BUST IN AND THRASH HIM WITHIN AN INCH OF HIS LIFE?
BECAUSE---IT'S BATHLESS GROGGINS!!!
OHO! WE UNDERSTAND!!!

YES, EVERYBODY IN TOWN KNOWS THAT BATHLESS IS PRACTICALLY A DEAD MAN—EVERYBODY BUT BATHLESS HIMSELF!!!
IT'S BEEN (SOB) MIGHTY WHITE O' EVERYBODY TO COOPERATE WITH ME IN MAKIN' POOR BATHLESS' LAST 30 DAYS ON EARTH HIS HAPPIEST-BEIN' THAT IT WAS ME AS CAUSED THAT TRAGEDY!!!

BELIEVE ME, CO-OPERATIN' UNDER THESE CIRCUMSTANCES IS ALMOST MORE THAN FLESH AND BLOOD CAN STAND!!!
YOU WON'T HAVE TO STAND IT MUCH LONGER, JASPER. TOMORROW AFTERNOON AT PRECISELY 3 O'CLOCK COMES---THE END!!!

THE NEXT AFTERNOON-A MINUTE OR TWO BEFORE THREE. YOU'RE SURE, PROFESSOR, THAT WITHIN TWO MINUTES POOR OLD BATHLESS WILL DISINTEGRATE BEFORE OUR VERY EYES?
THERE'S NO POWER ON EARTH THAT CAN STOP IT---

LITTLE DID HE REALIZE THAT WITHIN THAT GINGER-ALE BOTTLE, WHICH I LEFT IN YOUR OFFICE, BUD, WAS H-2347, A LIQUID THAT WITHIN 30 DAYS, IF TAKEN INTERNALLY, COMPLETELY DISSOLVES THE HUMAN FRAME!!!
IT WAS (SOB) MY FAULT FOR NOT WARNIN' HIM WHEN I LEFT HIM IN MY OFFICE WITH THAT BOTTLE!!!

THAT'S WHY I'VE SPENT THOUSANDS WITHIN' THE LAST 30 DAYS ARRANGING THAT ANYTHING BATHLESS WANTED IN THIS TOWN WAS TO BE GIVEN HIM FOR FREE, WITH ME PAYIN' THE BILLS!!!
AHEM!!! PROFESSOR-HE SHOULD HAVE DISINTEGRATED 10 MINUTES AGO!!!
PRECISELY!!! I CAN'T UNDERSTAND IT!!! HE'S STILL IN ONE PIECE!!!

•A HALF HOUR LATER•
WHY DOESN'T HE DO WHAT HE'S SUPPOSED TO DO---NAMELY, DISINTEGRATE BEFORE OUR VERY EYES?
HE'S SEEN US!!! HE'S-HE'S LAUGHIN' AT US!!!
Copr. 1945 by United Feature Syndicate, Inc.
Tm. Reg. U. S. Pat. Off.—All rights reserved
2-18

WAITIN' FOR SOMETHIN', BOYS?---LIKE MAYBE FOR YOUR OLD PAL TO DISINTEGRATE BEFORE YOUR HORROR-STRUCK EYES?
YES, FRANKLY-THAT'S EXACTLY WHAT WE'VE BEEN WAITING FOR!!!

WELL, YOU MIGHT'S WELL GO HOME!!!---I WASN'T CHUMP ENOUGH TO DRINK THAT BOTTLE OF H-2347-NOT AFTER ME HAVIN' BEEN JANITOR AT THE CHEMISTRY LABORATORY A COUPLA YEARS AGO!!!
THEN-YOU KNEW ALL THE TIME YOU WERE MAKING A SUCKER OF ME?

KEERECT!!! AND THANK YOU, BUD, FOR ALL THEM FREE MEALS, MOVIES, SEEGARS, POOL GAMES, CLOTHES- AND THANK YOU, JASPER, FOR THE MANY HAPPY DATES WITH YOUR FIANCÉE, WOWEEE!!! WHATA RED-HOT MAMMA!!!
GROANN
I WISH I WAS DEAD!!!

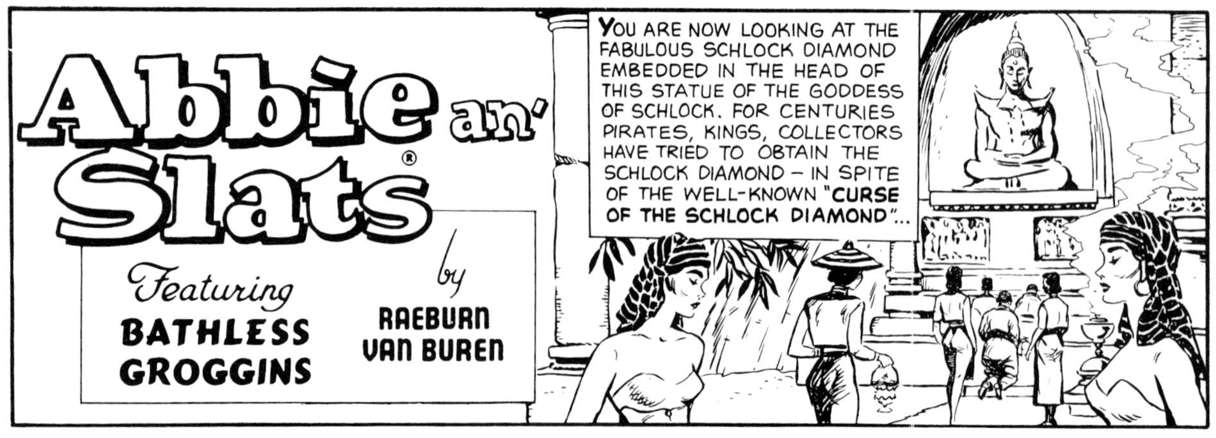
Abbie an' Slats
Featuring BATHLESS GROGGINS
by RAEBURN VAN BUREN
YOU ARE NOW LOOKING AT THE FABULOUS SCHLOCK DIAMOND EMBEDDED IN THE HEAD OF THIS STATUE OF THE GODDESS OF SCHLOCK. FOR CENTURIES PIRATES, KINGS, COLLECTORS HAVE TRIED TO OBTAIN THE SCHLOCK DIAMOND — IN SPITE OF THE WELL-KNOWN "CURSE OF THE SCHLOCK DIAMOND"...

MY COLLECTION OF THE RAREST JEWELS IN THE WORLD IS COMPLETE EXCEPT FOR ONE — THE SCHLOCK DIAMOND! I, HAMISH KITE, MUST OWN IT!
EVEN BIGGER CON MEN 'N ME HAVE TRIED T'GET THEIR HOOKS ON THE SCHLOCK DIAMOND, MR. KITE —

— AND THEY'RE NEVER HEARD FROM AGAIN — ONCE THEY GET WITHIN' GRABBIN' DISTANCE O' THE SCHLOCK IDOL!

MONEY'S NO OBJECT, GROGGINS. I'LL REWARD YOU RICHLY FOR THE SCHLOCK DIAMOND — ONLY I MUST (SOB) HAVE IT!

THEY TELLS ME THE BABES GUARDING THE SCHLOCK DIAMOND AIN'T ARMED WITH NOTHIN' MORE THAN A SMILE!
Tm. Reg. U. S. Pat Off.—All rights reserved
Copr. 1958 by United Feature Syndicate, Inc.
R. VAN BUREN

SEEMS LIKE ALL YOU NEEDS IS A LADDER AND A LITTLE KNOW-HOW, AND THAT HUNK O' ICE IS MY TICKET T' (CHUCKLE) A LIFE O' EASE. PROVIDED, (SHUDDER) THE CURSE O' THE SCHLOCK DIAMOND DON'T LOUSE THINGS UP!
10-12
TO BE CONTINUED

BATHLESS HAS BEEN ASSIGNED BY THE FAMOUS JEWEL COLLECTOR— HAMISH KITE— TO GET THE ACCURSED SCHLOCK DIAMOND!
WHAT BEATS ME IS HOW THEM DELICATE-LOOKIN' TOMATOES HAS BEEN ABLE T'KEEP CROOKS LIKE ME FROM WALKIN' RIGHT UP AND COPPIN' THE SCHLOCK ROCK— JUST FOR THE REACHIN'!

IT'S PLAIN T'SEE THEY AIN'T WEARIN' ENOUGH CLOTHES T' CARRY CONCEALED WEAPONS ON 'EM!

ALL YOU GOT T'DO IS SASHAY RIGHT UP T' THE IDOL AN'—AN'—
WOULDST SHARE A PERSIMMON-ADE WITH ME— YOU WITH THE MAJESTIC NOSE OF A WHOOPING CRANE?

THE SCHLOCK DIAMOND KIN WAIT, TOOTSIE, TILL YOU AND ME ORDERS ANOTHER ONE O' THESE TIME BOMBS, HUH?

AS IT HAS WAITED LO THESE MANY CENTURIES IT CAN WAIT ANOTHER FEW BRIEF MOMENTS, BATHLESS OF GROGGINS!
HIC!

SUDDENLY I (YAWN) FEELS AN' OVERWHELMIN' YEN T'-- (YAWN) HIT-- THE-- HAY--
HE HAS BEEN PERSIMMONIZED, HEDY!

UTTERLY!!

WHEN HE REGAINS CONSCIOUSNESS HIS MIND WILL BE A BLANK— ALL KNOWLEDGE OF THE SCHLOCK DIAMOND WILL BE OBLITERATED!

AND THUS ANOTHER THREAT TO OUR JEWEL AMONG JEWELS HAS BEEN ELIMINATED!

THAT'S WHAT YOU THINK, GIRLS--- NOT KNOWIN' THAT A GROGGINS HAS GOT A BUILT-IN RESISTANCE T' PERSIMMON-ADE. NOW (CHUCKLE) T'GET MY ITCHIN' HANDS ON THAT HUNK O' ICE!
R.VAN BUREN
10-19
TO BE CONTINUED

ON AN ASSIGNMENT FROM THE FAMOUS JEWEL COLLECTOR, HAMISH KITE, BATHLESS IS ABOUT TO LIFT THE FABULOUS (BUT CURSED) SCHLOCK DIAMOND!
THIS IS (CHUCKLE) LIKE TAKIN' CANDY FROM A BABY!

HE IS ALMOST THERE!

FINDERS KEEPERS, GIRLS —
THE DIAMOND IS NOT YOUR SOLE REWARD, OH NIMBLE ONE WITH THE FACE OF A WALRUS —

YOU MEAN I GETS A BONUS FER SWIPIN' YOUR ROCK?
IT IS WRITTEN IN THE SACRED BOOK, THAT HE WHO POSSESSES THE DIAMOND —

— DESERVES THE RICHEST AWARD — RICHER BY FAR THAN THE POOR BAUBLE YOU HOLD IN YOUR HAND —
MEANIN' EXACTLY WHAT, KIDDO?

— THE HAND OF CHIEF — OUR PEERLESS LEADER — IN MARRIAGE!
EXCUSE ME FER BEIN' NOSY, GIRLS —

BUT DOES THIS BOSS O' YOURS LOOK ANYTHING LIKE YOU KIDS?

SHE IS THE GREATEST OF US ALL!
THE MOST OF THE MOST!

THEN WHAT'RE WE WASTIN' TIME FER? LEAD ME BACK T' THIS TOMATO! FER THE FIRST TIME IN YEARS I (CHUCKLE) FEELS A MATRIMONIAL ITCH!
10-26
R. VAN BUREN
TO BE CONTINUED

BATHLESS GROGGINS NOT ONLY COPPED THE SCHLOCK DIAMOND, HE'S GETTING A BONUS—THE HAND OF THE MAIDENS' CHIEF IN MARRIAGE!
THIS IS LIKE SCORIN' A DOUBLE BULL'S-EYE! WHEN DO I GET A PEEP AT THE LUCKY TOMATO WHO'S GONNA BE MRS. BATHLESS GROGGINS?

SOON!

HOLD ON, KITTEN!
IT IS PART OF THE CEREMONY, ANOINTED ONE—YOUR GIFT TO YOUR WIFE-TO-BE. WHEN YOU ARE JOINED, EVERYTHING SHE OWNS BECOMES YOURS—

WELL, IN THAT CASE LET HER HOLD IT FER A COUPLA MINUTES!

YOU MAY LOOK NOW—
I KIN FEEL GOOSE PIMPLES GETTIN' BUMPS ALL (GASP) ON THEIR OWN!

HELLO—(GASP!!) SOMEONE'S BEEN (SHUDDER) TAMPERIN' WITH THAT FACE!

—WITH A MALLET— KING (UGH)-SIZED!

THERE'S SOME THING'S A MAN'LL DO FOR A BUCK—BUT GETTIN' HITCHED T' THAT WALKIN' HAUNT, NEVER!

MEN ARE (SIGH) SUCH COWARDS—THEY PREFER THEIR FREEDOM TO THE RICHES THE SCHLOCK DIAMOND CAN GIVE THEM!
AND LUCKY FOR US THEY DO!
11-2
R. VAN BUREN

ABBIE an' SLATS by
RAEBURN VAN BUREN

FRITZ VON SLITZ
AN INTERNATIONAL PROBLEM CHILD!
THE FAMOUS DUELIST, WHO RECENTLY SLEW HIS 100TH OPPONENT, HAS BEEN ORDERED DEPORTED FROM HIS NATIVE BULLGRAVIA, BUT THERE IS NO PLACE TO DEPORT HIM TO! THUS FAR, NO CITIZEN OF ANY OTHER COUNTRY HAS OFFERED TO SPONSOR HIS ENTRANCE.
FRITZ VON SLITZ

NEW YORK
BOSTON
LONDON
PARIS
INTER-OCEAN CABLE
TO— THE MINISTER OF PUBLIC SAFETY, BULLGRAVIA
IF YOU WILL RELEASE FRITZ VON SLITZ TO MY CUSTODY, I WILL ACCEPT FULL RESPONSIBILITY. HAVE IMPORTANT PUBLIC RELATIONS JOB HERE THAT ONLY HE CAN HANDLE.
JASPER HAGSTONE
CRABTREE CORNERS
U.S.A.

THE MINISTRY OF PUBLIC SAFETY IN FARAWAY BULLGRAVIA
ACH! DOSE VOOLISH HAMERICANS! BUT-- IF HE VANTS DIS MAD KILLER HE CAN HAF HIM—UNDT I VASH HIM FROM MY HANDTS OFF!

ONE WEEK LATER
HERR HAGSTONE, NO?
CLICK!

MY RELATIONS WITH ONE PARTICULAR MEMBER OF THE AMERICAN PUBLIC, GROGGINS BY NAME, ARE NOT SATISFACTORY. THE MOST UNSATISFACTORY THING ABOUT GROGGINS IS THAT HE IS ALIVE!
HERR HAGSTONE! I AM NOT A CHEAP MURDERER. I DO NOT KILL PEOPLE FOR MONEY LIKE A HIRED ASSASSIN! I KILL ONLY THOSE WHO OFFEND ME!

BUT FOR ONE THOUSANDS DOLLARS AMERICAN CASH MONEY I COULD BE VERY EASILY OFFENDED!
SPLENDID! NOW GROGGINS IS A TYPE WHO WOULD NEVER GO TO THE POLICE TO SETTLE ANY PRIVATE QUARREL! HE'S THE RUGGED INDIVIDUAL TYPE WHO'D PREFER TO SETTLE THAT SORT OF THING PERSONALLY, HIMSELF!

HA! I AM FAMILIAR WITH THAT TYPE! I HAVE LEFT 100 OF THEM SLICED TO RIBBONS ON THE DUELING FIELDS OF EUROPE! ALL HE HAS TO DO IS INSULT ME!
AND ALL YOU HAVE TO DO IS TO BE IN HIS VICINITY FOR A WHILE AND YOU'LL BE INSULTED, ALL RIGHT!

HERE'S FIVE HUNDRED NOW. FIVE HUNDRED MORE WHEN YOU HAVE SUCCESSFULLY DEFENDED YOUR HONOR AGAINST GROGGINS' FOUL INSULT!
AND INSULT ME HE WILL! THE UNCOUTH SWINE! ON THAT YOU HAVE MY WORD OF HONOR AS A BULLGRAVIAN GENTLEMAN!
CLICK!
9-15
R. VAN BUREN
TO BE CONTINUED

$500 NOW — AND $500 MORE, VON SLITZ, WHEN YOU PAY GROGGINS FOR HIS VILE INSULTS!
AND INSULT ME HE WILL, I ASSURE YOU! IT'LL BE EASY TO BE INSULTED FOR ONE THOUSAND DOLLARS, AMERICAN CASH!

THE SKILL OF FRITZ VON SLITZ IS STILL SUPREME!
SWISH!
SWISH!
THAT DERBY COST ME 20 DOLLARS BUT IT'S BEEN WORTH IT, REALIZING THAT'S GOING TO HAPPEN TO GROGGINS!

AHH—YES! THIS IS WHERE I WAS INFORMED THE SWINE GROGGINS HANGS OUT!
BUD TEAGLE'S POOL AND BILLIARDS

QUIET, EVERYBODY! THIS IS FOR THE CHAMPION-SHIP — AND TWO DOLLARS CASH!

BUMP!
RRRIP!

YA SLOPPY BABOON!
SPLENDID! HE HAS JUST SIGNED HIS DEATH WARRANT! NOW TO REMOVE MY GLOVE, SLAP HIM IN TH' FACE WITH IT, SEND IT TO THE LAUNDRY AND TH' DUEL IS ON!

ONE SIDE!
9-22

CRASH!
Copr. 1946 by United Feature Syndicate, Inc.
Tm. Reg. U. S. Pat. Off.—All rights reserved
R. VAN BUREN

SO WHAT IF HE DID BUMP MY ELBOW? HE DIDN'T MEAN NOTHIN' BY IT! YOU DIDN'T HAVE NO RIGHT T' GIVE HIM THAT DIRTY LOOK!

YOU'RE A STRANGER HERE AND I'M GONNA SEE YOU GET TREATED COURTEOUSLY. MY NAME'S GROGGINS!
TO BE CONTINUED

FRITZ VON SLITZ, DEADLIEST DUELIST OF ALL MITTELEUROPA, COLD-BLOODED EXTERMINATOR OF ONE HUNDRED HONORABLE OPPONENTS, REPORTS TO HIS AMERICAN "ANGEL," JASPER HAGSTONE.

YES, HERR HAGSTONE, I MET THE SWINE GROGGINS!
CLICK!
SPLENDID! AND NATURALLY YOU INSULTED HIM AND ARRANGED FOR THE MUR---OOPS— I MEAN THE (CHUCKLE!) DUEL?

NOT EXACTLY. I INSULTED HIM, OF COURSE, BUT THE STUPID OLD GOAT MISUNDERSTOOD. HE CONSIDERED MY INSULT AN ACT OF FRIENDSHIP!
LET'S HAVE NO MORE OF THIS FRIENDSHIP NONSENSE!

THIS IS A BUSINESS ARRANGEMENT! YOU MUST ARRANGE TO GIVE GROGGINS THE BUSINESS!
BEFORE THIS DAY IS DONE — A DUEL WILL BE ARRANGED!

THIS TIME HE WILL NOT MISUNDERSTAND. WHO COULD MISUNDERSTAND A DELIBERATE SLAP IN THE FACE?
THE DIRECT APPROACH! THAT'S IT, VON SLITZ!

AND IF YOU DO IT IN PUBLIC IT WILL BE EVEN MORE HUMILIATING! HMMM — TWO O'CLOCK! YOU'LL FIND GROGGINS HAVING HIS AFTERNOON FISH CHOWDER AT HARVEY'S FISH AND CHIP HOUSE!
I GO!

HA!
HARVEY'S FISH & CHIPS HOUSE

GROGGINS! DO NOT MISUNDERSTAND THIS!

BLAP!
Copr. 1946 by United Feature Syndicate, Inc.
Tm. Reg. U. S. Pat. Off.—All rights reserved
9-29

THANK YOU, PAL! I DON'T MISUNDERSTAND! NO ONE ELSE IN TH' JOINT HAD BRAINS ENOUGH T' SEE I WAS CHOKIN' ON THAT FISHBONE. YOU SAVED MY LIFE!
TO BE CONTINUED

WELL, VON SLITZ, HAVE YOU ARRANGED TO MUR--ER-I MEAN--DUEL WITH GROGGINS?
NOT EXACTLY, HERR HAGSTONE. IT'S A DIFFICULT CASE. I'M AN HONORABLE MAN. I NEVER KILL---ER-I MEAN--DUEL WITH AN OPPONENT UNLESS I INSULT HIM FIRST. TWICE I INSULTED GROGGINS!

--AND TWICE HE MISUNDERSTOOD ME! THE IRONIC RESULT IS THAT I HAVE BECOME A CLOSE BOSOM FRIEND TO THAT SWINE!
VON SLITZ! I HAVE ALREADY ORDERED A BLACK ARMBAND FROM MY TAILOR--

--AND I WANT TO WEAR IT! SAVVY, VON SLITZ?
I ASSURE YOU THERE WILL BE NO MISTAKE THIS TIME! YOU MAY CONSIDER GROGGINS A DEAD MAN! I GO NOW TO INSULT HIM IN UNMISTAKABLE TERMS!

GROGGINS! YOU ARE A FILTHY, UNWASHED, REPULSIVE OLD BEAST!
HOLD MY CUE, CHARLIE!

YOU'RE TH' FIRST MAN THAT EVER HAD THE COURAGE T' SAY THAT T' ME, BUB! AN' YOU WERE RIGHT—EVERY WORD OF IT! I AM FILTHY AN' UNWASHED!

I AM A REPULSIVE OLD BEAST! NOBODY EVER CARED ENOUGH ABOUT ME T' POINT THAT OUT T' ME BEFORE. I ALLUS SAY, A MAN CAN TELL A REAL FRIEND--

--BY TH' FRANKNESS WITH WHICH HE SPEAKS! YOUR WORDS HAVE MADE A GREAT IMPRESSION ON ME, MATEY! AN' I CERTAINLY WILL WASH — ONE O' THESE DAYS!
BUD TEAGL POOL & BILLARD

JUST KEEP REMINDIN' ME OF IT FROM TIME T' TIME. WANNA GET IN TH' GAME?
NO, THANK YOU — I GO!
CLICK!

THERE'S A TRUE PAL! HE'D NEVER KEEP IT TO HISSELF THAT HE CONSIDERS ME A DIRTY OLE BUM! HE COMES RIGHT OUT AN' SAYS IT TO MY FACE!
10-6

AS FOR YOU BILGE-RATS! YOU PROB'LY SAY TH' SAME THINGS BEHIND MY BACK!
SOCK!
TO BE CONTINUED

SO, VON SLITZ—AGAIN YOU FAILED TO INVEIGLE BATHLESS GROGGINS INTO A DUEL! YOU MAY BE THE DEADLIEST SWORDSMAN IN ALL MITTEL-EUROPA — BUT BRAINS YOU HAVE— NIX!
I COULD SLICE HIM LIKE A BALONEY IF ONLY I COULD FIND SOME EXCUSE TO CHALLENGE HIM!

HMM—I HAVE AN IDEA! TONIGHT'S THE ANNUAL MEETING OF THE FORMER FIGHTERS FOR FREEDOM! WAR VETS, YOU KNOW---

I-ER-NEVER WAS IN UNIFORM EXACTLY—BUT I'VE FOUGHT MANY A BITTER BATTLE ON THE WAR CONTRACT FRONT. ALWAYS GOT THE HIGHEST PRICES!
I CAN SEE YOU WERE A GREAT PATRIOT, HERR HAGSTONE IF THERE WERE ONLY A FEW MORE LIKE YOU— WE'D HAVE WON THE WAR!

FLATTERY WILL GET YOU NOWHERE! LET'S GET DOWN TO BUSINESS! NOW AT SOME POINT IN EVERY MEETING, BATHLESS GROGGINS INEVITABLY HURLS A LOUD AND VILE INSULT AT ME! USUALLY I IGNORE IT---

THIS TIME, HOWEVER, HIS INSULT WILL NOT BE IGNORED. YOU WILL BE WAITING OUTSIDE THE DOOR!

WHEN YOU HEAR A LOUD, DISGUSTING VOICE ROARING OUT A LOW INSULT — YOU BURST IN AND SAY --

--"I DEMAND SATISFACTION ON THE FIELD OF HONOR FROM THE SCOUNDREL WHO JUST INSULTED MY DEAREST FRIEND"!
I HAVE TO REFER TO YOU AS MY "DEAREST FRIEND"? IN PUBLIC? FOR ONLY $500! ACHHHH!

MY DERBY! YOU LOATHSOME LOW-LIVERED SCUM OF THE SEVEN SEAS!!
Copr. 1946 by United Feature Syndicate, Inc.
Tm. Reg. U. S. Pat. Off.—All rights reserved
10-13

I DEMAND SATISFACTION ON THE FIELD OF HONOR FROM THE SCOUNDREL WHO JUST INSULTED MY DEAREST FRIEND!!
H-HE MEANS YOU, JASPER! TH' WHOLE TOWN'S HEARD THE CHALLENGE. YOU CAN'T BACK OUT!
GROANNNN!
SO I'M YOUR DEARES' FRIEND, HUH, BUB? MIGHTY NICE O' YOU T' SAY THAT. I USUALLY ENJOYS BATTIN' OLE HAGSTONE AROUND MESELF— BUT I'M NO HAWG. THIS ONE IS YOURS!
TO BE CONTINUED

VON SLITZ! YOU MAY BE THE GREATEST SWORDSMAN IN ALL EUROPE—BUT YOU ARE THE BIGGEST FOOL IN THE WORLD ALSO. BY A STUPID MISTAKE YOU'VE CHALLENGED NOT GROGGINS BUT ME TO A DUEL IN PUBLIC!

ONLY WAY I CAN SAVE MY FACE IS FOR YOU TO LEAVE CRABTREE CORNERS IMMEDIATELY!
I MAY BE A CROOK IN EVERY OTHER WAY, HERR HAGSTONE, BUT WHEN IT COMES TO DUELS, I HAVE THE SOUL OF HONOR!

I HAVE CHALLENGED YOU IN PUBLIC! BRIBERY WILL GET YOU NOWHERE! I WILL NOT CHANGE MY MIND!
Y-YOU MEAN YOU INTEND TO GO THROUGH WITH IT?

ALL CRABTREE CORNERS WILL BE WAITING AT THE PICNIC GROUNDS AT DAWN—TO SEE IF YOU DARE SHOW YOUR FACE. I WILL BE THERE, TOO, HAGSTONE!
(GROANNN!)

IF I DON'T TURN UP--I'LL BE BRANDED AS A COWARD! I'LL BE THE LAUGHING STOCK OF THE TOWN!

BUT..HMM ???—VON SLITZ IS A GREAT DUELLIST—HE KNOWS I AM THE MEREST NOVICE. HE WOULDN'T KILL ME IN COLD BLOOD! HE JUST COULDN'T! HE WON'T BE THERE. OF COURSE HE WON'T!

·DAWN·
YOU AREN'T THERE ARE YOU, VON SLITZ?
I CERTAINLY AM, HAGSTONE!

I'M HELPLESS! Y-YOU W-WOULDN'T M-MURDER AN INNOCENT MAN, WOULD YOU, VON SLITZ?
OH, WOULDN'T I, NOW?
10-20
R. VAN BUREN

BAM!
Copr. 1946 by United Feature Syndicate, Inc.
Tm. Reg. U. S. Pat. Off.—All rights reserved

WHAM!

Y-YOU SAVED MY LIFE, GROGGINS! AND I ALWAYS THOUGHT YOU HATED ME!
KEERECT. I DO! I HATE YE TOO MUCH T' LOSE YE! IF YOU WAS GONE THERE'D BE NOBODY T' BASH AROUND, INSULT, AN' HUMILIATE. WITHOUT YOU LIFE WOULD BE TOO EMPTY!

Abbie an' Slats
Featuring
BATHLESS GROGGINS
by
RAEBURN VAN BUREN
BATHLESS GROGGINS IS IN PARIS
THIS CHARACTER, CHARLES, SURE COPPED HIMSELF A BIG HIGH-UP IN GOVERNMENT. FUNNY, I NEVER CAUGHT HIS LAST NAME.

HOTEL
CHARLES SAYS I'M T' GET IN TOUCH WITH SASCHA THE ROBIN, THE WORLD'S MOST (PANT) BEAUTIFUL AND (SHUDDER) DANGEROUS WOMAN SPY. HE SAID SHE'LL TELL ME WHAT I'M SUPPOSED T' DO!

HERE IT IS — SASCHA, ON THE THIRD FLOOR. WAIT A MINUTE --!!

THERE ARE (GULP) TWO SASCHAS! ONE ON THE THIRD FLOOR AND ONE ON THE FOURTH FLOOR. GUESS I'LL TRY THE FOURTH-FLOOR SASCHA FIRST!

Tm. Reg. U. S. Pat Off.—All rights reserved
Copr. 1964 by United Feature Syndicate Inc.

SASCHA? I WAS SENT HERE BY CHARLES!
OH---
R. VAN BUREN

--YOU WANT SASCHA, THE SPY. SHE'S ON THE THIRD FLOOR!

YES, I AM SASCHA, THE MOST BEAUTIFUL AND DANGEROUS WOMAN SPY IN THE BUSINESS. COME IN, IF YOU PLEASE!
I (QUIVER) PLEASE!
5-24
TO BE CONTINUED.

THIS CHARLES CHARACTER SAYS I'M T' TAKE ORDERS FROM YOU, SASCHA THE ROBIN, MOST BEAUTIFUL AND DANGEROUS SPY IN THE BUSINESS!
ATTEND ME WELL, PIERRE THE FACELESS. WHAT I AM ABOUT TO PROPOSE WILL TAKE NERVES OF STEEL!

I'M ONLY (GASP) FLESH AN' BLOOD, SISTER!

YOU RECOGNIZE THIS PAINTING? IT IS THE MONA LISA AND IS BEYOND A DOUBT THE MOST FAMOUS — AND VALUABLE — PAINTING IN THE WORLD!
SURE LOOKS LIKE THE ORIGINAL!

THAT IS BECAUSE — IT IS THE ORIGINAL!
IT IS!!

·LATER·
NOW THAT YER FINISHED MY PICTURE, WHAT NEXT?
YOU WILL SEE, PIERRE THE FACELESS!

NOW I PLACE THE ORIGINAL MONA LISA ON THE EASEL -- TAKE MY PORTRAIT OF YOUR HEAD -- AND VOILA!!

IS THIS A GAG, SISTER?
A GAG? DOES THREE MILLION DOLLARS SOUND LIKE A GAG TO YOU? YOU SEE, MY COLLEAGUE, WE ARE ABOUT TO SMUGGLE THE GREAT MONA LISA OUT OF THIS COUNTRY!
P. VAN BUREN
5-31   Tm. Reg. U. S. Pat Off.—All rights reserved
Copr. 1964 by United Feature Syndicate, Inc.
TO BE CONTINUED·

SWIPE THE MONA (GASP) LISA!!
BUT IT IS NOT THE MONA LISA, MY FACELESS FRIEND. IT IS A PORTRAIT OF YOU IN YOUR ROLE AS AN ECCENTRIC MILLIONAIRE COLLECTOR OF SELF-PORTRAITS!

THAT'S WHAT I ALWAYS HAD A HANKERIN' FOR T' BE — AN ECCENTRIC MILLIONAIRE!

YOU WILL LEAVE THIS COUNTRY WITH YOUR CURIOUS PORTRAIT. ONCE YOU HAVE REACHED YOUR DESTINATION, I WILL BE AWAITING YOU. AND VOILA--

-- WE ZIP OFF YOUR FACE AND WE HAVE THE PRICELESS PORTRAIT OF MONA LISA READY TO GO TO THE HIGHEST BIDDER!

.MBER, PIERRE THE FACELESS, .HALL BE WAITING .HEN YOU ARRIVE. GUARD THE PORTRAIT WITH YOUR LIFE!
WITH MY LIFE? KEERECT! WHAT HAVE I GOT TO LOSE??
S.S.

NOW TO GET SOME SHUT-EYE!

LOOK OUT - WE'RE BEING RAMMED!!
CRASH

WELL (YAWN), TIME T' GET UP AND TIE ON THE FEED BAG. UMMM--- THIS BUNK SURE IS SOFT AND COMFORTABLE. LIKE SLEEPIN' ON WATER!
TO BE CONTINUED.

THE FAMOUS LOUVRE MUSEUM IN PARIS WHERE A CELEBRATED GIRL BY THE NAME OF MONA LISA USED TO HANG AROUND ---
THIS CALLS FOR STERN EMERGENCY MEASURES!
IT IS GONE!! MONA LISA HAS (GASP) BEEN PURLOINED!!
IT IS A NATIONAL DISASTER! THE ECONOMY WILL BE DESTROYED!

WHAT (SOB) WILL WE DO?

IF I AIN'T DEAD OR DREAMIN' THEN I'M SHIPWRECKED AND FLOATIN' AROUND THE DRINK WITH NOTHIN' BETWEEN ME AND DAVY JONES'S LOCKER EXCEPT A PICTURE O' MONA LISA THAT'S GOT MY FACE SUBSTITUTED FOR HERS!

MEANWHILE, BACK AT THE LOUVRE.
SHOULD THE NEWS THAT WE HAVE LOST MONA LISA SLIP OUT, HEADS WILL ROLL!
THEN PERHAPS MY IDEA HAS SOME MERIT!

SUBSTITUTE THIS COPY OF THE GREAT MONA UNTIL WE CAN REPLACE IT WITH THE ORIGINAL! AFTER ALL, WE ARE THE EXPERTS AND IF WE ALL ATTEST THAT THIS IS THE ORIGINAL – WHO CAN ARGUE WITH US?
WHO INDEED?! HANG IT, GASTON. YOU HAVE SAVED THE REPUBLIC FROM DISASTER!

ME WANT HIM!
Tm. Reg. U. S. Pat Off.—All rights reserved
Copr. 1964 by United Feature Syndicate, Inc.

ME MALUKAI FATS, QUEEN OF ISLAND. YOU SKINNY, BUT I LIKE YOU!

AND THAT'S WHY THE MONA LISA YOU SEE HANGING IN THE LOUVRE IS A MERE SUBSTITUTE FOR THE ORIGINAL, WHICH HANGS IN A LITTLE GRASS HUT SOMEWHERE IN THE SOUTH PACIFIC!! ANY QUESTIONS??
R. VAN BUREN
6-14

Abbie an' Slats
Featuring BATHLESS GROGGINS
by RAEBURN VAN BUREN
WHEN THE BANKRUPT SHEIK OF SHOLCKISTAN MIXED SOME (UGH!) SHEEPSKIN WITH A BOTTLE OF A POPULAR SOFT DRINK— BURPLE— THE RESULT WAS FABULOUS!!
NOW (SLURP) THIS SLOP HAS (UMMM) BODY!!
WHATEVER IT WAS THAT SHIEK SLIPPED INTO OUR BOTTLE OF (BURP!) BURPLE, HE'S IMPROVED THE TASTE A THOUSAND PERCENT!

WE MUST SEND REPRESENTATIVES IMMEDIATELY TO SHOLCKISTAN— AND BUY UP THE FORMULA OF THE INGREDIENT THIS SHEIK IS SPIKING BURPLE WITH!

A COUPLE OF DAYS LATER
THE SHOLCKISTANIANS SPEAK A DIALECT KNOWN ONLY TO ONE AMERICAN, CHIEF—
GET HIM— AND NEVER MIND THE EXPENSE!

THEM BURPLE FOLKS WANT ME T' TAKE A TRIP T' SHOLCKISTAN T' TALK MY OLD PAL, THE SHEIK, INTA SELLING SOME DRINK FORMULA HE DEVELOPS!

I GOT A NOTION BUZZIN' AROUND IN MY BRAIN—SOME KIND O' PROMISE THE SHEIK MAKES WHEN I LAST SEES HIM. MAYBE IT'LL COME T'ME LATER ON!

WHAT WAS THE PROMISE HE MAKES T'ME!! THE WORD "HEAD" KEEPS POPPIN' UP— BUT THAT'S ALL (SIGH) I CAN RECOLLECT!
GRABTREE CORNER

THE BURPLE MAKERS ARE SENDING A REPRESENTATIVE TO SHOLCKISTAN TO DISCUSS THE SALE OF OUR FORMULA TO THEM!
WHO IS IT, ALL-KNOWING ONE?

IT IS—BATHLESS GROGGINS!! THE UNWASHED VILLAIN WHO SWINDLED ME OUT OF MY LAST RUPEE. IT WAS THEN I PROMISED BY MY ANCESTORS THAT—

—THAT I WOULD REMOVE HIS UGLY HEAD FROM HIS MISSHAPEN BODY SHOULD HE EVER SET FOOT IN MY COUNTRY AGAIN!
12-1
SO THAT'S (SHUDDER) IT!! MORE NEXT WEEK!

SENT TO NEGOTIATE FOR THE SHEIK OF SHOLCKISTAN'S SECRET "BURPLE" FORMULA, BATHLESS GROGGINS REMEMBERS IT'S WORTH HIS (SHUDDER) HEAD TO REVISIT THIS COUNTRY!
SINCE (CHUCKLE) FORTY YEARS HAVE GONE BY SINCE I CONNED HIS NIBS OUT O' HIS LAST RUPEES...
SHOE POLISH

HE OUGHTA EXPECT—

ME T'AGE SO WHEN I SHOWS UP LOOKING LIKE THIS—HE'S GONNA SWALLER MY LINE THAT I'M NOT THE CROOKED CONFIDENCE CHARACTER HE FLIPS TO, BUT--

I'M J. PIERPONT GROGGINS JR., AS HONEST AS HIS OLD MAN WAS LARCENOUS! HERE'S HOPIN' HIS NIBS HAS LOST SOME O' HIS VISION!
S.S.N

TAKE YER GREASY PAWS OFF ME, BUSTER! I AIN'T WHO YOU THINKS I AM!
MASTER SAYS BRING YOU—IN PART OR IN WHOLE. CHOICE UP TO YOU!

AT LAST, GROGGINS THE THIEF—GROGGINS THE SWINDLER—GROGGINS THE SLIMY CHEAT—
HOLD YOUR CAMELS, SHEIK—THAT'S MY (CHOKE) LATE, SAINTED FATHER YOU'RE REFERRIN' TO!

YOUR (GASP) FATHER!! 'TIS TRUE—THE THIEF, SWINDLER AND CHEAT I REFER TO SHOULD BE A MUCH OLDER AND GRAYER MAN—
NOW YER TALKIN'! I'M THE SON O' THE MAN YER DESCRIBING—EVEN YOU CAN SEE THAT!

A THOUSAND PARDONS, SON OF GROGGINS THE THIEF, SWINDLER AND CHEAT—AND MY REMORSE AT HIS UNTIMELY END—
UNTIMELY—BUT I FIGGERS YOU HATED HIS GUTS, SHEIK?

UNTIMELY ONLY BECAUSE HE DIED A PEACEFUL DEATH, NOT AT MY REVENGING HANDS!
12-8

LUCKY FER ME YOU DON'T NURSE A GRUDGE, PAL.
ALL IS FORGIVEN, SON OF GROGGINS—AS SOON AS YOU PASS THE TEST!
WHAT TEST? CONTINUED NEXT WEEK

BATHLESS GROGGINS HAS CONNED THE SHEIK OF SHOLCKISTAN INTO BELIEVING THAT HE IS HIS OWN SON!!
SO BE IT, SON OF GROGGINS, THE THIEF AND SWINDLER — YOU ARE NOW TO TAKE THE TEST WHICH WILL PROVE WHETHER YOU ARE FRIEND OR ENEMY TO ME AND MY PEOPLE!

SHOOT, PAL!

BEHIND ONE OF THESE DOORS IS AN OPEN CAGE OF RAVENOUS LIONS --
RAVENOUS -? (GASP) DON'T THAT MEAN HUNGRY??

BEHIND ANOTHER OF THESE DOORS ARE SEVERAL BEAUTIFUL GIRLS —
THAT'S A (CHUCKLE) IMPROVEMENT!

BUT I SEES THREE DOORS — WHAT'S BEHIND THE THIRD?
A SURPRISE, GROGGINS, THE SON OF A SWINDLER — UNKNOWN QUANTITY!

AND YOU ARE TO ENTER ONE OF THEM. ARE THERE ANY QUESTIONS?
KEERECT — WHICH IS THE WAY OUT O' THIS JOINT?

THERE IS NO WAY OUT — SAVE THROUGH ONE OF THOSE DOORS! CHOOSE!

IF EVER THERE WAS A TIME FER YOU T' GET LUCKY, PAL — THIS IS IT!

WELL, WHICH DOOR WILL BATHLESS GROGGINS OPEN?
12-15
VAN BUREN
TO BE CONTINUED

DISGUISED AS HIS OWN SON, BATHLESS CAN ESCAPE FROM SHOLCKISTAN ONLY THROUGH ONE OF THESE THREE DOORS!
ONE'S GOT TIGERS BEHIND IT, ONE'S LOADED WITH BEAUTIFUL TOMATOES—
—AND THE THIRD HAS A (CHUCKLE) SURPRISE, SON OF THE UNWASHED SWINDLER GROGGINS!

WHICH WILL HE CHOOSE?

YOU CAN'T LIVE FOREVER, THEY TELLS ME—BUT THERE'S NO HARM IN TRYIN'!

WHICH'LL IT BE? THE (CHOKE) TIGERS, THE DAMES OR THE (SHUDDER) SURPRISE?

THE ANSWER'S COMIN' UP! DO I RUN, SET—OR WISHT I WAS NEVER BORN?

WHICH DOOR DID THE SON OF THE UNSANITARY GROGGINS CHOOSE, ALL KNOWING ONE?

LISTEN CAREFULLY FOR THE SOUND OF HIS VOICE—THAT WILL REVEAL ALL!
(Tm. Reg. U. S. Pat Off.—All rights reserved
Copr. 1957 by United Feature Syndicate, Inc.

NO!!

GROGGINS, SON OF THE UNBATHED ONE, HAS CHOSEN THE DOOR LEADING TO THE (SIGH) UNKNOWN QUANTITY!!
R. VAN BUREN
12-22
SURE—BUT WHAT IS THE UNKNOWN QUANTITY?? MORE NEXT WEEK!!

BATHLESS GROGGINS HAS OPENED THE DOOR WHICH LEADS TO AN UNKNOWN QUANTITY---WHICH TURNS OUT TO BE--
A (GROAN) BLARSTED BATH-TUB FULL O' CHURNIN,' FOAMIN' WATER!

AND THE ONLY WAY OUT IS (GASP) THROUGH IT!!

DON'T OPEN THAT DOOR—IT LEADS TO THE (SHUDDER) TIGERS!

I GETS MY CHERCE, DON'T I? O.K. I'M A YELLER-BELLIED COWARD, I ADMITS IT!
SQUEAK!!

I'M TAKING THE EASY WAY OUT!

IT'S (QUIVER) AN' OL' TIGER HABIT—LICKIN' THE VICTIM CLEAN BEFORE THEY RENDS 'EM LIMB FROM LIMB!!

THERE'S SOMETHIN' REVOLTIN'LY FAMILIAR ABOUT (SNIFF) THIS CAT—IT'S (GASP) BEULAH!

THE OL' GAL REMEMBERS ME FROM THE LAST TIME I WAS HERE AND WON HER HEART BY FEEDIN' HER STEAK-RARE-EVERY DAY!
PURRRR-R-R-R--
P. VAN BUREN
12-29

IS IT OVER, ALL-KNOWING ONE?
THE TIGERS ARE UNDOUBT-EDLY FINISHING THEIR (CHUCKLE) LAST MORSEL OF GROGGINS, RARE!

YOU ARE ON A RARE-STEAK DIET THE REST O' YOUR NATURAL LIFE, BEULAH, OL' PAL! IT'S SMALL ENOUGH PAYMENT FOR SAVIN' ME FROM THE HIDEOUS FATE O' TAKIN' A BATH!
Tm. Reg. U. S. Pat Off.—All rights reserved
Copr. 1957 by United Feature Syndicate, Inc.